Advanced Praise for
Developing Tomorrow's Leaders Today
Insights from Corporate India

I believe that the only useful knowledge is one that is personal, and meaningful learning comes only from personal experience, especially in the behavioral domain. *Developing Tomorrow's Leaders Today* presents stories that can trigger self-reflection and thus start the unfolding of lessons of experience. I was delighted to read the book, and have been guided by the experiences of others presented in the book. Meena Surie Wilson offers us the *Panchatantra* of leadership, and it will find its way in organizations effortlessly—simply through word-of-mouth. It is a gem that will shine on anybody's book shelf.

Dharm P. S. Bhawuk
Professor of Management and Culture and Community Psychology
Shidler College of Business, University of Hawaii, Manoa

Making things happen in India follows different rules and this book takes us to the source of solutions—to the masters who made things happen.

Devdutt Pattanaik
Chief Belief Officer, Future Group

Developing Tomorrow's Leaders Today is rich and insightful in more ways than one. Meaningful experiences shared in the form of stories make the book very easy to read and the personal assessment tools help readers to reflect and take stock of their strengths and weaknesses. It marries rich CCL research and frameworks with Indian managerial experiences and insights. I found it be very useful to discover my own strengths and weaknesses and highly recommend it.

Prasad Kaipa
CEO Advisor and Coach
Visiting Fellow, Center for Creative Leadership

How do we help leaders improve execution skills or even help improve their confidence? How do we sharpen their ability to be innovative and build entrepreneurship? These are common development dilemmas that leaders face. *Developing Tomorrow's Leaders Today* identifies seven such experiences that can help leaders learn 11 important lessons. A great book with clear and insightful takeaways that address the "how-to" in developing leaders.

Abhijit Bhaduri
Chief Learning Officer, Wipro Limited

Developing Tomorrow's Leaders Today provides readers with impactful insights on the Indian model of leadership development. An outstanding book with clear guidelines given using the "opportunity matrix of seven unique experiences and 11 lessons", based on real-life stories of successful professional Indian Leaders and capturing the rich hues of Indian culture and ethos. A must read for CEOs and all HR professionals keen on developing tomorrow's leaders.

Dr. Prakash V. Bhide
President, Corporate HR, JK Organization (EZ), India

The ultimate limit to the growth and sustainability of any enterprise is the quality and capacity of its leadership. Meena Surie Wilson provides us with stories from real-life experiences of senior business leaders in India. Any organization or individual interested in improving their quality of leadership will find the additional guidance—for self-assessments, reflections, and thoughtful conversation—very useful.

G. V. Prasad
Vice Chairman and CEO, Dr. Reddy's Laboratories

Developing Tomorrow's Leaders Today

Insights from Corporate India

Developing Tomorrow's Leaders Today

Insights from Corporate India

Meena Surie Wilson

JOSSEY-BASS
A Wiley Imprint
www.josseybass.com

Center for Creative Leadership
www.ccl.org

This edition is published in 2010 by John Wiley & Sons (Asia) Pte. Ltd., 2 Clementi Loop, #02-01, Singapore 129809 on behalf of Jossey-Bass, A Wiley Imprint, 989 Market Street, San Francisco, CA 94103-1741–www.josseybass.com

Jossey-Bass books and products are available through most bookstores. To contact Jossey-Bass directly, call our Customer Care Department within the US at 800-956-7739, outside the US at 317-572-3986, or fax 317-572-4002.

Jossey-Bass also publishes its books in a variety of electronic formats. Some content that appears in print may not be available in electronic books.

Library of Congress Cataloging-in-Publication Data

ISBN: 978-0-470-82568-6

Typeset in 12/15pt, Goudy by Thomson Digital, India

Printed in Singapore by Saik Wah Press Pte. Ltd.

10 9 8 7 6 5 4 3 2 1

Dedicated to all who inspire me:
My only son, affectionate family,
delightful colleagues, and good friends

Contents

Acknowledgments

A heartfelt "thank you" to all who have contributed, supported, nudged, and conspired to bring this book to the light of day. I would especially like to thank Mr. Satish Pradhan and Mr. Radhakrishnan Nair of the Tata Group for their early sponsorship of the research. Without Mr. Satish Pradhan championing the project by recruiting companies to participate, creating a research unit at Tata Management Training Center, and allocating additional resources as needed, this book would not exist.

The following companies have agreed to be publicly recognized for participating in this landmark study: Dr. Reddy's, ICICI Bank, ITC Ltd., JK Organisation (Eastern Zone), Mahindra & Mahindra Ltd., and the Tata Group, including Tata Chemicals and Tata Steel. Many thanks for your early vote of confidence. To the senior leaders from corporate India who consented to share precious time and memories, and the HR professionals who made the interviews possible, your contributions are the heart of this book. I cannot thank you enough.

Dear *Lessons of Experience—India* research team—Corey Criswell, Sangeeta Mathur, Abinash Panda, Ellen Van Velsor, Rola (Ruohong) Wei, Jeff Yip, and Yi Zhang—we owe each other a debt of gratitude for all we have accomplished together. Serena Wong: I appreciate your hours of analysis, writing, and thoughtful contributions to chapter 2.

Dave Altman, Jennifer Martineau, Michael Jenkins, and Ellen Van Velsor: this achievement is due to your sponsorship, warm personal support, and push to "get it done!" Many thanks!

My gratitude to those who have lent support to the final phase: Cindy McCauley, one of the Center's pioneers on "learning from experience," for her comments; Karen Lewis from the CCL Publications Group, for assistance with the manuscript; and Jules Yap, Fiona Wong, and Nick Wallwork from John Wiley & Sons (Asia) Pte. Ltd. for professional oversight. Nick: *gracias* for your admirable patience, good humor, and lasting faith in this CCL project.

Finally, for your creative contributions to my thinking and writing—Peter Scisco, Anupam Sirbhaiya, Lyndon Rego, Jeff Yip, Anand Chandrasekar, and Kavita Neelakantan—words cannot convey my thankfulness. Kavita and Anand: Kudos also for your hours of devoted work that have made this publication possible, with a *dhanyavad* to Kavita for connecting the findings to its implications for Indian managers. On our behalf, I offer an invocation for continued blessings from Ganesha, divine remover of obstacles, so that this book may serve its readers well.

About the Author

Meena Surie Wilson is a senior enterprise associate with the research, innovation, and product development group of the Center for Creative Leadership–Asia Pacific (CCL–APAC). Meena joined CCL in 1992 as a research associate. She is currently based in Jamshedpur, India.

Meena's most recent assignment as research director for the CCL–APAC office in Singapore involved starting up a research unit to advance knowledge about leadership development in countries in Asia. Previously, as interim managing director, CCL–Asia, and director, Asia-Pacific Relations, Meena completed a special assignment to launch the CCL–Asia office in Singapore in July 2003. She worked with an enterprise team to open up the new office, develop networks, and explore alliances with international partners.

Meena's research has focused on learning leadership from experience, and cross-cultural managerial effectiveness. A published author, her credits include chapters on "Learning from Experience" in *The Center for Creative Leadership Handbook of Leadership Development* third edition (Jossey-Bass, 2010); "Foundations of Responsible Leadership: From Self-Insight to Integrity and Altruism" in *Handbook of Responsible Leadership and Governance in Global Business* (Edward Elgar, 2005); "Effective Cross-Cultural Leadership: Tips and Techniques for Developing Capacity" in *Crossing Cultures: Insights from Master Teachers* (Routledge, 2004); and "Leading Across Cultures:

Five Vital Capabilities," which appeared in *The Organization of the Future* (Jossey-Bass, 1998). Meena is lead author of *International Success: Selecting, Developing, and Supporting Expatriate Managers* (CCL, 1998) and *Managing across Cultures: a Learning Framework* (CCL, 1996).

In addition, Meena facilitates assessment, feedback, and coaching modules included in several CCL programs, and contributes to the design and delivery of conference modules and workshops. A native of India and a former resident of Alaska, her previous work experiences include educational policy analysis for the state of Alaska, program development for public schools in Anchorage, Alaska, and project work at the Xavier Labor Relations Institute in Jamshedpur, India.

Meena completed her undergraduate studies at Mills College in Oakland, California, and holds an M.S. degree from Syracuse University in television–radio journalism and a Ph.D. in adult and organizational development from UNC-Chapel Hill.

Foreword

A major challenge is that views are often formed and held with little or no data to bring people to hold them.

This book is refreshing and amazing because it presents data and facts based on interviews. And, happily, the interviews cover an excellent cross-section of people, and bring out both experiences and lessons learned—leadership lessons.

The author and her colleagues are to be complimented in presenting issues simply, clearly and, on one topic, leadership—which is just very important for everyone because leadership is relevant at every level, not just at the top. There is very little clarity on this subject.

Experience truly shapes leaders; most of all, failure is the best learning experience. Early success on the other hand can lead to complacency, overconfidence, and a short-term approach. There are different experiences to have, and whether they succeed or fail, people can learn from their experiences.

Currently, if one looks at the Indian situation in particular, leadership has to cover not only running a company or an organization very well, but also looking beyond to community and social responsibility and action. What is demanded from leaders is therefore very complex.

But there does not need to be a shortage of leadership talent. Leadership is not the exclusive domain of a few. Even ordinary people are capable of extraordinary achievement, given opportunities (to learn to lead), trust, and space. In this book, we see the listing of experiences and lessons based on research, data, analysis, and learning. From all of this comes strategy and action.

The story of leadership is the story of running a marathon, not a hundred-meter race. Experience leads to learning and lessons, and this process goes on and on. A good leader evolves with experience, learning to motivate people, discipline people, and to extract achievement and application.

Meena Surie Wilson is to be congratulated for bringing out a bunch of key lessons for tomorrow's leaders in corporate India, who can make an enormous contribution to building and running conscious and competitive corporates, which are now playing a central role in India's development and growth.

Tarun Das
President, Aspen Institute India
Former Chief Mentor, Confederation of Indian Industry (CII)
August 2010

Preface

The year 2006 marked a milestone—for the Center for Creative Leadership (CCL) and for me personally. With the endorsement of CCL's board of governors and support from the Singapore Economic Development Board (SEDB), CCL launched an Asia-based research unit. With this, CCL's continuing commitment to benefit society worldwide merged with the hopes and dreams of a small group of CCL researchers, including me.

As background, CCL established its Asia-Pacific (CCL–APAC) office in Singapore in 2003. In 2009, CCL opened an office in Pune, India. From both these bases, CCL expected to offer a portfolio of products and services to serve global and regional clients. The portfolio would include the leadership development programs and interventions for which CCL has an established reputation worldwide, as a top-10-ranked executive education provider.

The 2006 decision to launch the first research unit outside North America was momentous. Since its inception in 1970 in Greensboro, North Carolina, CCL's employees have taken pride in its research-based nonprofit educational charter. Although CCL has grown from 10 associates in North Carolina to several hundred associates in Asia, Europe, North America, and Russia, and although its programs are offered every year to more than 25,000 leaders around the globe, CCL continues to honor its research roots. The prospect of starting a research unit in Asia was especially exciting: CCL's tradition of using research to anchor leadership development would be carried forward in another region of the world.

The mandate for the initial team of eight researchers (Jeff Yip, Chris Ernst, Vijayan Munusamy, Patricia O'Connor, Anand Chandrasekar, Rola Wei, Yi Zhang, and me) came from the Center's senior leaders, the vision of David Altman, then the vice president for Research and Innovation, and key members of his team including Jean Leslie, Jennifer Martineau, Marian Ruderman, and Ellen Van Velsor. The initiative was blessed by CCL's board of governors and then president, John Alexander.

Professionally and personally, I was excited about the broad mandate to start up a research unit. What an extraordinary opportunity to reconnect not just with leadership development professionals in Asia, but specifically in India, where I had grown up! I had joined CCL as a researcher in 1992, and served in a variety of roles. Between 1999 and 2003, I had worked with a team to explore where to establish our first office in Asia. That was followed by my leading the team responsible for opening the Singapore office. But this was different. This was a chance to collaborate with Asian researchers, and to learn about regional leadership development issues with them and from them. We would be using an Asian lens to produce knowledge about leadership and leadership development.

As a first step, three research initiatives were designed carefully. These were the *Leadership Gap* study (GAP), *the Bridging Cultural Boundaries* project (BCB), and the *Lessons of Experience* (LOE) program of research. Well-grounded research is resource intensive. We were fortunate to be welcomed and given material and moral support by leading institutions in India, Singapore, and China—the Tata Management Training Centre (TMTC) in Pune, thanks to the auspices of Mr. Satish Pradhan; the Civil Service College (CSC) in Singapore due to the personal involvement of Mr. Paul Lim; and the Leadership Behavioral Laboratory at the China Europe International Business School (CEIBS-LBL) in Shanghai via the contributions of Professor Jean Lee. Our collaborators helped us in many ways—by providing access to organizations and interviewees or survey respondents; by committing researchers to work alongside us through the lengthy process of data collection, analysis, and interpretation; and by giving administrative support.

Well-grounded research takes time. For those who are interested, a query to CCL at info@ccl.org or a visit to the CCL website at http://www.ccl.org/leadership/research/projects.aspx will showcase that during the past few years, each of the three projects has advanced knowledge and laid the foundation for ongoing research in Asian countries. In this book, I am highlighting the *Lessons of Experience—India* (LOE–India) research, on which I served as principal investigator.

WHY STUDY HOW EXECUTIVES LEARN AND DEVELOP?

A central question has provoked the interest of researchers and educators at the CCL for more than 30 years: how do executives learn and develop over the course of their careers? The question arises naturally from wanting to know how managers become effective leaders.

Guided by this curiosity, the LOE studies were initiated in the U.S. in the early 1980s to investigate executive learning and development. As the managerial ranks in the U.S. became more diverse and began to include women, African-Americans, Hispanics, and Asian-Americans, additional studies were designed to investigate their experiences and lessons learned. Outside of CCL, the same research methodology was applied to examine the experiences of international executives and business executives in the Netherlands and Japan. In 2003, CCL extended the LOE research globally, with comparable interview and survey data gathered from more than 500 senior leaders in 47 country-based organizations across seven industry sectors in the U.S., India, Singapore, and China.

Considerable investments have been made over four decades to obtain insights into what and how executives learn from experience. Within a few years of joining CCL, I too wanted to know more about how Indian business leaders learn to be effective. Would their developmental path be similar to or different from that of senior leaders in the U.S. and other countries? That is why I felt lucky to be asked to implement the LOE research in India, Singapore, and China. I was especially grateful when CCL reached an agreement with TMTC to launch the LOE–India research as one of a suite of cooperative projects. Conducting my first interview for the LOE–India study in July 2006 was a personally momentous occasion.

LESSONS OF EXPERIENCE—INDIA RESEARCH PROJECT: A SNAPSHOT

Completed in 2008, the LOE–India research provides clear and extensive insights into how Indian business leaders develop over time. The critical incident technique adapted for the study has proved enormously useful. Key events, or experiences that drive learning and change, have been identified. Through these experiences, executives learn leadership lessons. Their learning generates a shift in attitudes, values, knowledge, skills or behavior, thereby making them more effective as business leaders. In this study, 309 experiences were gathered, with 572 lessons produced by the experiences.

A team of four researchers, including myself, collected and analyzed the interviews. These research colleagues are India-based and Indian. I am of Indian origin, have been based in the U.S. and Singapore, and after more than 40 years, am living in India once again. Each of us pored over pages of transcribed interviews scrupulously, garnering the experiences and learning reported by the business executives. Then we came together to achieve consensus about the nature of the executives' experiences and the essence of their leadership learning.

The TMTC team—Abinash Panda, Chitra Duvedi, and Sangeeta Mathur—were originally based in Pune and have now moved on to other assignments. Their cooperation, enthusiasm, and weeks of labor during the early phases of this project were invaluable. Subsequently, my colleagues and I at CCL have focused on the implications of the research for Indian companies. We have analyzed the data to uncover the link between experiences and lessons learned. Why is this important?

The propositions underlying this book are that leadership ability is not inherited or genetic; nor is it developed in classroom settings from coursework or in mid-career training programs. Instead, leadership skills emerge from experiences; and different experiences are needed to sharpen different leadership skills. These are not new propositions. But given the rapidly evolving business environment in India, and the urgent need for more leaders and more proficient leaders, what could be as important as knowing what are the most critical leadership lessons to learn, and which experiences teach those lessons?

Findings from the study are shared in the chapters that follow. To set the context, here is a brief review of how the climate for business growth has changed and the implications for leader development.

THE CHANGING PROFILE OF THE BUSINESS ENVIRONMENT IN INDIA

There have been radical and rapid changes in the Indian business context since independence in 1947. At that time, national leaders placed their faith in economic socialism, wanting the new India to be economically self-sufficient. Although moderate and steady growth occurred in the 1950s, the economy sputtered in the next two decades. To support infrastructure and economic development, the government increasingly had to rely on an infusion of loans from international agencies.

Then the international oil crisis triggered the 1991 balance of payment currency crisis in India. Foreign exchange reserves were depleted due to international borrowing. Indian goods and services were of poor quality and not competitive in the global marketplace. In response, the government committed to economic liberalization.

The early 1990s were watershed years. Monetary, fiscal, international trade and exchange rate, and industrial policies were reformed comprehensively. These policies created a more competitive environment that improved efficiency and productivity and enabled Indian companies to enter the international market.

Since then, economic growth in India has achieved a turnaround. In recent years, India's role as a driver of worldwide economic growth (with Brazil, Russia, and China or the BRIC countries) has been recognized. With one of the world's fastest-growing economies as a base, many Indian businesses are running to take their place on the global stage. India is poised for future business growth. The situation demands a new kind of leader at all levels. Can the leadership talent needed to run behemoth organizations be developed as quickly as needed?

As a result of this research, we now know more about the most important leadership lessons that Indian business executives must grasp; and we can identify the experiences from which these lessons can come. But knowledge is never enough. The more difficult next step is how to translate knowledge into actionable scenarios that organizations can implement. Can Indian leadership talent be developed as quickly as needed? For now, the answer is: "Yes, possibly." We need to imagine how leadership at all levels can invigorate Indian organizations; and we need to craft an experiential curriculum that points future managers toward the leadership lessons they need to succeed. I trust this book will be one step on the journey ahead.

Meena S. Wilson
August 2010
Jamshedpur, India

1

SEIZING THE MOMENT—LEARNING FROM EXPERIENCES

> I will begin with the importance of learning from experience. It is less important, I believe, where you start. It is more important how and what you learn. If the quality of the learning is high, the development gradient is steep; and given time, you can find yourself in a previously unattainable place.
>
> —*N. R. Narayana Murthy,*
> *Chief Mentor, Chairman, Infosys Technologies*[1]

This is a tumultuous time for Indian businesses. For those aspiring to be tomorrow's business leaders, the challenges ahead are formidable. Globalization is creating intense pressures on leaders worldwide and redefining what is demanded of them. This force is also keenly felt in India, where the country's top business leaders tackle thorny, yet promising opportunities for business growth daily. This book proposes pathways for future top executives to prepare themselves, by learning to use experiences to become ever more effective as leaders.

No longer is it wise to depend solely on leadership programs and formal coursework. Aspiring leaders must learn continuously, which is why there is so much power in learning to learn from experience. Most of us spend the bulk of our lives and most of our daily hours at work. Every type of experience teaches specific leadership lessons. But which experiences carry the most lessons? And what are the lessons that are most important to learn to succeed as a business leader in India? Fundamental answers to these important questions are found in the pages of this book.

We start with two real-life stories that show just how much impact work experiences have on shaping the manager's ideas and actions. The stories describe assignments undertaken by Mr. Parikh and Mr. Venkat. (The names are pseudonyms but the stories are true.) Each was at the forefront of creating change, and through his experience, learned much about leading.

Then you are presented with an *Opportunity Matrix* (see table 1.1) and the schematic *Seven Experiences, 11 Lessons: Pathways to Leader Development* (see figure 1.1). Each displays the knowledge generated by the study in formats that can be used easily by leaders and potential leaders. Based on interviews with more than a hundred senior executives from Indian business organizations, the Opportunity Matrix showcases how experiences are learning opportunities and links managers' experiences with the lessons they learned. The good news is that different experiences teach different lessons, and from many different experiences, many leadership lessons can be learned.

For readers who prefer a bird's-eye view, *Seven Experiences, 11 Lessons* provides a structure for developing tomorrow's Indian business leaders today. This schematic maps to the content in the book chapters and further simplifies the information in the Opportunity Matrix. If you are preparing yourself or others to be a leader, both the table and the figure pinpoint what the research tells us about the leadership abilities and skills that are the most important to develop, and the experiences from which you can source them.

As background, and for readers who are interested, I will briefly review the research project. Additional details about the study are included in the appendix. The chapter concludes with notes on how readers, like you, can best use the book to develop leadership in yourself and others.

STORIES OF EXPERIENCES AND LESSONS LEARNED

Here are two stories that illustrate how experiences generate learning. (As noted, pseudonyms are used in these and all the stories that follow. References to places and people have been changed to protect the identity of the interviewees and their companies.) In the first story, Mr. Parikh tries to change the ingrained attitudes of employees. He does so successfully. In the second story, Mr. Venkat challenges conventional notions of how to do business and rapidly increases the sales of his company's product. More important than their successes however, are the ways in which Mr. Parikh and Mr. Venkat develop as leaders—readying themselves for further growth.

Making Change Simple

Gokul Parikh was assigned to manage a factory that was facing problems on every front: operating expenses were exorbitant, outdated technologies were in use, workers completely lacked quality consciousness, union leaders often stirred up discontent, and productivity levels were abysmal. Despite agreement among top management that this factory could be a true asset to its company, conditions had continued to deteriorate for several years, and the idea of closing the operation started to gain momentum.

Mr. Parikh realized that even if the factory were to close, he and his management team would not lose their jobs because they would be absorbed elsewhere in the company. But he could not see his team or himself simply shrugging their shoulders and walking away. The team decided to turn the operation around.

Despite the history of contentious relationships with union leaders, Mr. Parikh confided in them and asked that they join his team's efforts to prevent the factory closing. They were unresponsive. "*Thik hai*, try your luck," they said, choosing to neither support nor oppose the team. So, after informed discussions, Mr. Parikh and his team opted to talk with the workforce directly. They pointed out that if productivity improved, the economy of that factory-based township would improve, the employees and their families would prosper; and the region's downward spiral toward poverty would halt.

Perhaps the workforce sensed that the management team had a sincere purpose. Or perhaps they were won over by their honest, transparent communications. They backed up the management team's plan of action completely. What they did not know was that the team had thoroughly analyzed the issues and determined the cause of the very low productivity. Absenteeism, exceeding 20 percent, was rampant! Key employees would simply not come to work—sometimes because they were not interested in earning more, and at other times because they were chasing other sources of income. With key employees absent, neither the machinery nor the factory ever operated properly. But if absenteeism could be brought down to 5 percent for just 12 months, productivity and quality would shoot up, costs would come down, and in Mr. Parikh's words, "the factory would look very, very good." Moreover, the team figured out that after a year, they could use a clause in the Industries Act and apply for a license to expand the factory by 25 percent; the bigger and better factory would then offer more jobs and create better economic conditions for the region.

So Mr. Parikh's team focused on controlling absenteeism. Their plan was stunning in its simplicity. Labor traveled to the factory from scattered regions. The management decided to organize 40–50-person groups by region. Each group would be handed a doable objective: "Make sure your neighbor comes to work every day." This was not complicated or difficult to understand. After each worker made sure that his or her neighbor came to work, his or her responsibility would end. He or she could be satisfied that he or she had been given an objective and achieved it. The team prepared its campaign and went to the workers.

After a two-month pilot, the campaign lasted for 12 months. The results were amazing: absenteeism fell below 6 percent and production grew from 75 percent to 125 percent of target. "You couldn't believe it was the same factory as 12 months ago," said Mr. Parikh, "and the effects were long lasting. After that, absenteeism never went back to the earlier levels!"

In retrospect, Mr. Parikh's main lesson learned was that even very complex issues can have simple solutions:

> I think our team was able to create this unity of purpose and also simplify the whole purpose. We didn't get into productivity and efficiency calculations. We set a very simple target that each team of 40–50 people would have to make sure that everybody came to work everyday. Employees realized that their families and they would benefit, since the growth of their factory would lead to the growth of their township.

Mr. Parikh believes that success came because the team's superordinate goal secured communitywide involvement. The workers were able to see that if they produced less, they would earn less. But if they succeeded at changing that, there would be better times ahead for everybody. Large-scale change, in this case, hinged on a simple idea that opened up a big change in workforce attitudes.

Business as Unusual

Bala Venkat headed up a sales territory of several districts, and was assigned to sell a product that was new at the time: compact fluorescent lamps (CFL). His company had a state-level contract for city lighting, and during an incidental conversation with state politicians, he was advised to consider using rural women's self-help groups to increase the sales volume of his new product. This seemed like a wild idea, but Mr. Venkat was willing to explore further. The door was opened for him to make a presentation to one of the more aggressive district collectors. The district collector (DC) was able in turn to introduce him to the rural women leaders who were anchoring social improvement work in the villages.

Mr. Venkat recognized that the politicians had a stake in addressing their state's enormous power shortage. Meanwhile, the DC had a development agenda for the villages. From Mr. Venkat's presentation, the politicians and the DC could see how 1 megawatt of power and 60 lakhs (a lakh is 100,000 rupees) could be saved annually per 50,000 CFLs sold. The DC also saw that the energy-saving campaign could become a part of the self-help agenda that the women's groups were already implementing with their literacy and cleanliness campaigns. On his part, Mr. Venkat saw an opportunity for the women to be a sales force for his company and become economically self-sufficient too.

The campaign scored many firsts. Schemes had to be created and details worked out. A sales force of 1,200 women was started. They were given sales commissions, with many earning money for the first time. They learned to do house-to-house demonstrations to compare ordinary bulbs with CFL lamps, using a kit developed by Mr. Venkat. A financial partner stepped forward to invest in the project by extending credit to the women for their initial purchase of the CFL lamps from Mr. Venkat's company. Passbooks were printed and issued so that each woman could record purchase and sale transactions. Mr. Venkat became completely involved, working alongside the women to watch the way they worked. From this, a quota of 48 lamps per saleswoman per monthly sales cycle was set, and a baseline for sales was established.

The campaign succeeded in unexpected ways, to the satisfaction of the women, the DC, the state's politicians, and Mr. Venkat and his company's top managers. His team was recognized at an international companywide quality competition and achieved a first place for the Asia-Pacific region. Several years later, when many more well-established multinational companies arrived on the scene, they flocked to learn how women's self-help groups could be deployed.

"Selling through a self-help group of women was a very wild idea," said Mr. Venkat. He emphasized that for breakthrough achievements, it was not always necessary to follow existing processes. New, unconventional ways could be worked out. But people, and your relationships with people, made a difference; and good ideas from your stakeholders had to be used, so that there was a combined effort to meet different agendas.

The experience had enormous personal impact on Mr. Venkat too. He resonated with the strong passion of the DC, who, quoting Nehru, asserted that "the life of India is in its villages." Mr. Venkat was humbled and moved by the enthusiasm of the women's self-help groups. He said:

> See, basically the women had no idea of the product or anything, they had no experience of selling, and they were not highly trained or educated. But they were eager because this was something new, and they felt that it is good for the country and good for them also to earn something. One of the ladies showed me the house-to-house demonstration they developed—switching between the two kinds of bulbs, and then going to read the meter the next day to show the energy savings. The ladies knew that "seeing is believing." I learned a lot from them.

Mr. Parikh and Mr. Venkat's experiences are only two of more than 300 experiences collected by interviewing senior Indian business executives. The lessons they learned are part of an extensive array of more than 500 leadership lessons. The following Opportunity Matrix synthesizes what we learned from interview analysis.

THE OPPORTUNITY MATRIX

The purpose of the Opportunity Matrix is to simplify the complex phenomenon of executive development without being simplistic. Several hundred stories were narrated by the senior business leaders. The variety of experiences and nuggets of leadership wisdom gleaned from their stories have been distilled into this matrix. We found that seven kinds of experience and 11 lessons, derived from those experiences, were described the most frequently. At CCL, we find it useful to cluster lessons into those related to leading self, leading others, and leading the business. The value of this model will be discussed in the final chapter.

An important caveat: managers' rich experiences at work and in life, and what is learned from experiences, cannot be encapsulated in a table with 11 rows and seven columns even when the table is derived from rigorous analysis. For example, our distillation of the data indicates that *confidence* can be learned from *bosses and superiors*, *turnarounds*, and *new initiatives*; but *confidence* is also boosted by other experiences. Similarly, according to our analysis, college graduates start to form *personal leadership insights* based on impressions collected on their *first professional job*; obviously however, a *first professional job* yields new learning on many fronts.

SEVEN EXPERIENCES, 11 LESSONS: PATHWAYS TO LEADER DEVELOPMENT

Based on a landmark study that uses a proven methodology and breaks new ground, *Seven Experiences, 11 Lessons* organizes essential findings so that busy leaders and managers can quickly access what they need to know about experiences and the leadership lessons they produce. "YOU" refers to the manager who is at the hub or center of experiences that fan out in front of him or her. The seven pathways of experience radiate, summoning managers to different courses of action. Past-generation managers have traveled along these paths,

Table 1.1 Opportunity Matrix: Experiences and leadership lessons learned

Leadership lessons learned ↓ / *Experiences* →	*Bosses and superiors*	*Creating change: Turnarounds*	*Creating change: New initiatives*	*Horizontal moves: job rotations and transitions*	*Cultural crossings*	*Increases in job scope*	*First professional job*
Leading self							
Confidence	X	X	X				
Self-awareness		X	X				
Personal leadership insights	X						X
Leading others							
Managing and motivating subordinates	X					X	
Developing subordinates	X						
Navigating politics and gaining influence			X				
Engaging with multiple stakeholders				X			
Cross-cultural savvy					X		
Leading the business							
Effective execution	X	X					
Innovation and entrepreneurship			X				
Functional and technical expertise			X	X		X	

Figure 1.1 ***Seven Experiences, 11 Lessons:*** **pathways to leader development**

learning imperative leadership lessons, and today's managers are invited to do so too. This array of 11 lessons has been carefully sifted from the detailed accounts given by the veteran leaders participating in the study.

The concept of *lokasamgraha*—variously translated from Sanskrit as "welfare of the world," "holding together the people," and "service to society"—arcs around the circumference. (Cognate words for *loka* are world, people, and society; and for *samgraha* are welfare, trusteeship, and service.) The desire to situate managerial work within the larger scheme of life goals and purpose is an implicit theme in the lives of Indian managers. The spirit that Indian business leaders bring to their undertakings resonates with *lokasamgraha*, which is a strong undercurrent in the Indian ethos.[2] This element of the schematic is introduced here and will be elaborated in the last chapter. The schematic itself is a high-level view; details and nuances are explained in chapters 2 through 8.

Note that there is a logical sequence in which the experiences are discussed (see figure 1.2). The experiences that were more frequently discussed in the interviews are presented first.

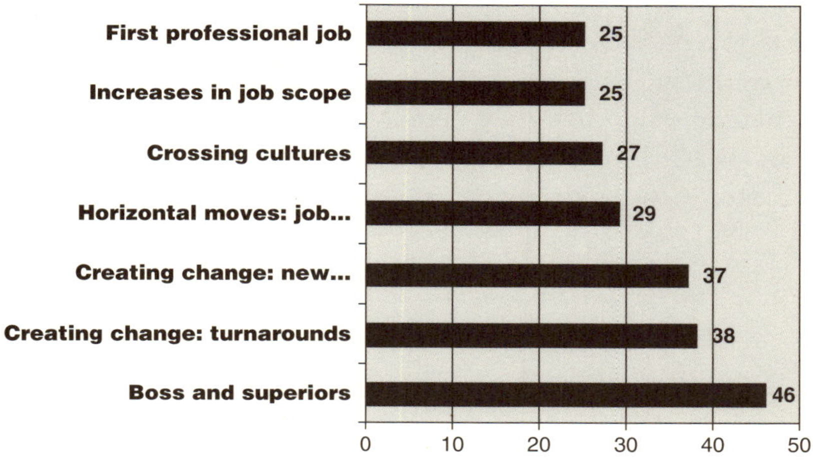

Figure 1.2 Seven essential experiences (based on percentage of interviewees who reported each experience)

For example, since 46 percent of Indian managers learn leadership lessons from their bosses, in comparison with 37 percent learning lessons from new initiatives, the chapter on bosses precedes the one on new initiatives.

HOW INDIAN BUSINESS EXECUTIVES LEARN AND DEVELOP: LAUNCHING THE INVESTIGATION

To explore what and how executives learn, we interviewed more than 100 senior-level Indian business leaders (see tables 1.2 and 1.3). Our interviewees were selected from eight Indian companies that have established themselves globally. These companies were intentionally chosen to represent various industries (manufacturing, banking and financial services, pharmaceuticals, and conglomerates) with organizational headquarters in all four corners of India.

From the senior executives, we heard stories of their first professional experience, promotions, transfers, special assignments and profoundly personal events. They shared their reflections on what they had learned, and how they had changed, on their way to becoming a successful leader in corporate India. By listening to, transcribing, and analyzing the rich narratives that they generously provided, the research team[3] was able to home in on the experiences that had enabled the executives to climb to the pinnacle of their careers and to

Table 1.2 Interviewees' seniority

Level	
President	9
CEO, MD, Dy. MD	10
Sr. VP, Exec VP, VP	13
COO, CE	9
SBU Head, Director	11
Sr. GM, Dy. GM, GM, AGM	19

Table 1.3 Demographics

Gender Male: 68 Female: 3	No. of companies: 8
Age < 50 yrs:39 > 50 yrs:32	Industry sectors • Manufacturing • Financial services • Pharmaceuticals • Conglomerate
Work experience > 15 years	

run businesses in India. The insights obtained from these corporate leaders about their paths of learning and growth are fascinating and instructive.

To gather their lessons of experience, we asked two questions:

- Looking back over your career, what are the three key events or experiences that had a lasting impact on you and influenced how you lead and manage today?
- What did you learn from these events or experiences?

The chapters offer you stories and quotations containing the practical wisdom that came from these top business leaders in response to our questions.

USING THE BOOK

This book is meant for men and women of action, such as yourself. If you are reading these words, either you wish to make progress on your own leadership journey or you wish to help others to go forward on theirs.

We all love stories. Our lives are full of stories or narratives of events that we have observed or experienced.[4] Of course, stories are colored by the storyteller's memory, powers of observation, projections, and imagination. Entertaining, instructional, juicy, factual, or persuasive—stories construct the way we view our world. Stories, revolving around major events in their career, are at the heart of managers' lives too.

In this book, the stories told by interviewees are used as vehicles for traversing the landscape of managerial careers in India-based global companies. For each of us, our own experiences are without doubt the best teacher. As Swami Vivekananda reminds us, "Knowledge can only be got in one way, the way of experience; there is no other way to know."[5] But for those on their way to becoming business leaders, these stories are a helpful way to absorb the hard-won lessons in leadership that today's senior business leaders have accrued from their lifetimes of experience.[6]

(Parenthetically, please note that my choice to represent the research accurately has limited the content of this book in some ways. For example, there are insufficient stories about senior women leaders. Moreover, my focus is on high-performing managers in general, not on the high-profile Indian business leaders who are repeatedly in the media spotlight with their doings and misdoings. Finally, if there is a leadership lesson that is not highlighted, that is because that lesson was not highlighted in the interviews.)

Each chapter calls on you to improve yourself as a leader. By reading the many stories and quotations, you are immersed in depth and vicariously in the lives of other leaders. The central lessons embedded in their experiences are described in detail too. This will ignite your own memories and provoke you to reflect more deeply on what your experiences have taught you. Frameworks are given and questions are asked to guide your introspection. A self-assessment is included to give you information about how well you have mastered a leadership lesson. You can then use the suggestions that follow to plan a course of action for self-improvement. We recommend that you start a log and write notes to yourself, because this will become a valuable journal documenting your leadership journey.

These pages offer a nontraditional perspective on the nuts and bolts of leader development. Grounded in four decades of research knowledge and practical experience with developing leaders, the Center for Creative Leadership (CCL®) view is that the artistry of effective leadership unfolds over time and calls for a different kind of hard work. This is the work of going inward to reflect on one's experiences, thoughts and feelings, what is being learned, and how the learning can be applied. The stories, frameworks, and exercises are all directed toward giving you inklings about who you want to be as a leader.

Recently, I read Gurcharan Das' aptly titled treatise *The Difficulty of Being Good: On the Subtle Art of Dharma*. I was struck by the extent to which the CCL perspective mirrors, as one example, Yudhishthira's leadership journey as told in the epic *Mahabharata*. This prince and ruler conscientiously struggled to be an effective leader, while remaining true to his own *dharmic* commitments. Here is a man who reflected on his experiences, values, and the counsel given him by others at every step.[7]

We expect that your reflection and note taking will be followed by your joining a small group of like-minded others, or even one other person, in meaningful conversations. The purpose of your multilogue or dialogue will be to cross-examine personal perspectives and opinions more objectively, and to share leadership expertise among a community of practitioners.

I believe that this book can especially benefit three groups of readers:

- Ambitious and tenacious young managers who aim to develop themselves and become effective and successful as leaders will find a roadmap for steering their careers. The knowledge shared in these pages can help them drive their way forward, through the managerial ranks and into the echelons of executive leadership.

- Senior executives aiming to develop the next rung of leaders can use this book as a springboard to form a sensible plan for cultivating future leaders. For many top leaders, a plan to develop the next generation of leaders has become a strategic necessity. A demonstrated commitment to developing leadership talent enables organizations to attract and retain the top talent who will steer their business in the future.
- All global executives (of both Indian and non-Indian firms operating in India) will be better prepared to form an HRD strategy and adjust their approach to leadership development in India. Any manager who is responsible for selecting and developing managers to work in India, or must work across cultures with Indian counterparts, will learn about how leadership is exercised in the Indian context. This book is not just for Indian managers; it is also about managing in India.

The leadership skills needed for tomorrow need to be cultivated today. The demand for high-caliber leaders, dispersed across levels and throughout an organization's global operations, clearly exceeds the supply. What compounds the supply–demand gap is the complexity of running large global businesses. This supply–demand gap challenges organizations to tackle leader development systematically and intentionally. Fortunately, there is a leader development curriculum that can quicken the maturation of managers into leaders. That curriculum is based on linking experiences to leadership learning. The knowledge to do so is available. In the words of the futurist and sociologist Alvin Toffler, "As we advance into the terra incognita of tomorrow, it is better to have a general and incomplete map, subject to revision and correction, than to have no map at all."[8]

ENDNOTES

1. N. R. Narayana Murthy. Pre-commencement lecture at the Stern School of Business New York University, May 9, 2007. Available at http://www.rediff.com/money/2007/may/28bspec.htm.
2. S. K. Chakraborty, *Ethics in Management: Vedantic Perspectives* (New Delhi, India: Oxford University Press, 1995).
3. The primary research team included Abinash Panda and Sangeeta Mathur from the Tata Management Training Center in Pune, and Meena Wilson from the Center for Creative Leadership–Asia Pacific in Singapore.
4. D. Pattnaik, *Everybody Tells a Story*. Available at http://devdutt.com/everybody-tells-a-story.
5. Vivekananda Vedanta Network, Ramakrishna Vedanta Society of Boston. Available at http://www.vivekananda.org/quotes.aspx.
6. A. Simmons, *Whoever Tells the Best Story Wins: How to Use Your Own Stories to Communicate with Power and Impact* (New York, NY: AMACOM, a division of American Management Association, 2007).
7. G. Das, *The Difficulty of Being Good: On the Subtle Art of Dharma* (New Delhi, India: Penguin Books India Pvt. Ltd., 2009).
8. A. Toffler, *Powershift: Knowledge, Wealth and Violence at the Edge of the 21st Century* (New York, NY: Bantam Books, 1990).

2

BOSSES WHO MAKE A DIFFERENCE

> The most important attribute a leader can possess is the ability to be teacher, coach and guide, the beacon that lights the path to wisdom.
>
> —*Mr. Muthuraman, former managing director, Tata Steel*[1]

As Mr. Muthuraman's words indicate, top leaders in India often expect to be a beacon to others and show them the way. Reciprocating their view, Indian subordinates typically expect to learn important lessons from bosses. In our interviews, bosses were the number one source of leadership learning, with 46 percent of senior executives recalling the impact of one or more bosses on how they behave now as leaders and managers. In countries such as India, with a strong tradition of learning from superiors and where title, status, and authority command respect and deference, the role of superiors in molding future leaders is unquestionable.

Bosses at all levels, knowingly and unknowingly, impart guidance and inspiration through their words and actions. Four prototypes emerge from analyzing the interviews. Bosses can be positive role models, negative role models, catalysts, and teachers. Prototypes are not meant to label a boss, but to point to four patterns of behavior among Indian bosses. Sometimes the same boss can be a positive model in some situations and a negative model in others. Or a boss can embody two prototypes by being, for example, both a positive role model and a teacher.

Over the course of your career, you have worked or will work with many bosses and superiors. Your relationships with each of them will be unique. The stories told about the four prototypical bosses will give you ideas about how to absorb the most learning possible from different bosses. There is a payoff to watching and learning from the many bosses whom you encounter over long hours and years of employment. Consciously or unconsciously, you will internalize their approach to managing and motivating subordinates. And at the time that you become a boss, your own experience as a subordinate comes full circle. This is when the learning that you have absorbed from your bosses manifests in how you manage your subordinates.

Though the ability to manage and motivate subordinates successfully is the foremost leadership lesson learned from bosses, there are other lessons that bosses impart. Catalyst and teacher bosses, for example, build self-confidence and demonstrate the importance of developing subordinates. Teacher bosses also proactively show their subordinates how to get a job done. And all bosses—by their actions and words—convey a philosophy about the role of the leader and the meaning of leadership.

To help you to understand different types of bosses and to absorb leadership lessons from them actively and intentionally, in-depth descriptions of the four boss prototypes follow.

THE POSITIVE ROLE MODEL

This boss or superior does not set him- or herself up to be a model for his or her subordinates. Yet how these bosses conduct themselves as leaders and managers makes them, in the eyes of their subordinates, examples of how to act (or how not to act, in the case of the negative role models described next). The junior managers may not even have interacted directly with their positive role model. Often, there is just the simple experience of observing the bosses in action. The impression that the bosses leave is the important factor. Their habits, and sometimes their small gestures, capture the imagination of the subordinates and become a source of inspiration.

This is illustrated by the two examples that follow. In each, how the teaching occurs is unpremeditated on the part of the boss, yet the lessons have a profound impact on his subordinate, motivating him to imitate his role model. In the first narrative, Mr. Nair sets an example of how to bring out the best from his people. He also demonstrates how to delegate effectively by developing trusting relationships. In the second narrative, Mr. Mahalingam makes his subordinates feel valued by his interest in their lives outside of work. In both examples, the bosses' behaviors motivate their subordinates to improve their performance.

Mr. Nair Leads by Example

By all accounts, Mr. Nair was not the most talented engineer in the company. But he was particularly good in relating to and managing people and this critical skill helped him consistently outperform the so-called hotshots in the company. For instance, he always went the extra mile. When any visitor left his office, he would open the door himself, go to the lift, and personally see him or her off. "My boss was in many respects an average person, but he was very good at keeping people happy," recalled Ram, who worked for Mr. Nair for several years. "I see other bosses who are more talented but are not able to get the best out of others."

Another lesson Ram learned from Mr. Nair was the importance of building trust. "I learned how when you do a project, the most valuable element or attribute is trust. You have to trust your people. Say you are running a very big contract and handling your project team and more than two dozen contractors, you can't be doing everything on your own and you have to build trust."

Mr. Mahalingam's Personal Touch

Rao was impressed by the way in which his boss Mr. Mahalingam connected with subordinates. The company had grown to 200 employees, but Mr. Mahalingam could still remember the names of the wives of the 200 managers. Rao said, "Some people just have that skill. Now, I don't have it, but I could feel the impact of something like that. You walk into a corporate party and the manager comes to you and instead of saying 'Mr. So-and-so, Mrs. So-and-so, how are you?' he says, 'How are you, Shanti, and how are the children? How is the young one doing—has he passed out of tenth class and how did he do in his exams?'"

Observing his boss's impact on people, Rao decided to emulate him. "I am not so good at remembering names, so I started designing a way," he said. "If I am going to have a meeting with my marketing boys in Mumbai, I make it a point to have my secretary get me the names of all the managers in the marketing department and their wives' names and so forth. So, by design, I use the same technique, though as a person I am not gifted like Mahalingam."

THE NEGATIVE ROLE MODEL

Here is a boss who behaves in ways that his or her subordinates find offensive. Often the encounter with negative role models is a one-on-one interaction in which the manager who is describing the experience is adversely affected by his or her boss' poor managerial behavior. Managers' descriptions of the negative role models who crossed their paths are vivid and emotional. But as you will see, even negative role models can have a constructive influence.

Two stories follow. In the first situation, the subordinate loses motivation when he is neither given credit nor recognized for his work. In the second situation, the subordinate becomes completely demotivated when he is publicly, rudely, and unfairly blamed for making a decision for which he was not privy to the relevant background information.

A Matter of Credit

Bhawuk was a freshly minted MBA, who expected to join the head office in Mumbai. But the company was going through financial setbacks, there were no open positions in Mumbai, and he was assigned to work in the smaller Kolkata office in corporate finance. To make him welcome, the senior managers in Mumbai had instructed his bosses in Kolkata to provide him with a satisfying work environment. This was not to be.

Bhawuk found that he was the only professional reporting in to a boss who took a dim view of his credentials since the Kolkata branch did not customarily hire MBA graduates. "There was an air of insecurity around the person to whom I started reporting. He was very particular about taking credit. Because I came from an MBA-granting institute, obviously my ability to put together a credit proposal was somewhat better, compared to that of some of the other people. So I was able to put together a comprehensive credit proposal. Then my boss would actually go out and say to the senior bosses in the head office, 'Look, this is the quality of the proposal that I am putting through.'"

At the time, Bhawuk didn't complain about this behavior. Instead, he told himself, "Fine. Every time the boss wants to take credit, let him take credit." Bhawuk had just stepped into a corporate world and its politics. As a result of his boss's actions, he started to distance himself emotionally from his boss and his work environment.

What he learned was how much it mattered to him that his work be valued. "Those lessons are still with me, and they're in the back of my mind forever. What struck me was how important it is for somebody to feel valued in an organization.

The key takeaway was that only if you feel valued in an organization will you will start giving that value back to the organization."

An Unbearable Bully

"Public humiliation is something a leader should never, never do but he was a guy who excelled in that. I was terribly upset and I still remember I had tears in my eyes. It was a traumatic experience."

Srini and 10 of his peers were in a boardroom review that was being conducted by the CEO. Srini had recently joined the company and was soaking in the sheer beauty of the room's natural setting and decor. Soon after the meeting started, he was startled to hear the CEO yelling at him, using offensive language. "There were other people present to whom I was a fairly senior person in the organization. I was so shocked. I just went out that boardroom and never came back. I went to my room. The experience was so painful because his facts were incorrect. I remember telling my colleague, 'I want to leave. I don't want to work here.'"

The issue revolved around a hiring decision that Srini had made that ran counter to what the CEO wanted. Using his best judgment, Srini had counseled a potential applicant to seek a position more suited to his qualifications. The discussion with the candidate had been very professional. What Srini had not been told was that favors were being exchanged, and the hiring decision was not his to make. For Srini, that was not the point. The point was that he was treated extremely disrespectfully by his boss, the CEO, which had never happened to him before.

A few days after the incident, the boss called him and apologized saying, "I understand you are very upset. I never meant all that." But the damage was done. In Srini's words, "On that day, he lost me as a leader. I am clear that I would never want to be a leader like him—never in my life. Nor will I ever work with a leader who is like that, not for all the money in the world."

THE CATALYST

The catalyst boss jolts his or her subordinate to perform at higher levels and take on bigger responsibilities. These bosses recognize that moving managers out of their comfort zone is an important way to develop future leaders. Like a muscle, the manager needs periods of stretch and strain to grow stronger. Years later, catalyst bosses are gratefully remembered for having taught subordinates to believe in themselves and developed their self-confidence. Here is what two managers said.

> My immediate boss told me very clearly, "Listen, you have progressed as far as you can in your career. Your next level should be to go and run a company. You can't just run bits and parts. The buck has to stop somewhere and it's got to stop with you and you have got to get that experience." So I landed in a new position and it was a very transformational experience.
>
> My MD called me because I was resisting a move to the HR department in the head office. I said that I was doing great in manufacturing and did not know much about HR. He said, "That is why we want you to come here. We want to give you a fresh look at HR. You will learn that way." And then he told me—and that is the first time he told me, "We think you have a potential to be in the top 20 of the company and if you don't prove yourself in two different functions and two different locations, we will not be able to consider you. Remain in manufacturing. But if you want to be on the board, you have to come to the head office and you have to prove yourself." Then I said okay.

Pushing subordinates to take on bigger challenges is only one of the ways in which catalyst bosses impart confidence and self-belief. The best catalyst bosses sense that subordinates do not just need challenging opportunities at critical points in their careers; they also need various kinds of support to be successful in meeting their challenge. So they provide sufficient autonomy, plenty of encouragement, and resources too. They often follow up by checking in and coaching the subordinate through the early days of a new role.

Overcoming Fears

A shy young manager who focused on his work to the point of isolating himself from his colleagues described what happened when he was put in charge of the entire credit portfolio for the zone, even though he was a raw officer.

> My boss knew that I am reserved. But as I was in charge of the credit of the entire zone, I needed to interact with people in the central office in Mumbai. So he made me do that. And not even that, he made me to talk to the general manager. He told me, "You talk, you present, you tell, and do not ever fear." That quality that he inculcated in me, I will never forget in my life. It remains with me till today. The trust he had! Till then, I did not at all have the confidence that I could deal with the general manager, who was four ranks higher than me, or that I would be able to impress him and convince him about what we wanted him to do and what decisions we wanted to get from him. From that day, I have been able to talk to anybody without any fear.

Making Decisions

Yet another way in which catalyst bosses help subordinates become self-assured is by letting them make their own decisions. A mid-30s manager who was running an online financial service business for her company heard that their competitors were about to launch a new service at a lower rate. She was traveling in the U.S. at the time, and got a call from her boss, who wanted to know whether a price war was likely. He asked her for her views, and they had a long candid discussion. But the way in which he concluded their conversation amazed her. "He simply said 'I trust you. Do what you think is best,'" she reminisced. "He did not give me a list of dos and don'ts or express any reservations about my ability to handle the situation." His unwavering faith in her allowed her to trust her own judgment and taught her to empower her people in the same way her boss had empowered her.

The approach used by catalyst bosses is nicely summarized by Azim Premji's comments on leading people to achieve more: "We give people major responsibilities even if they are only 60 percent ready. Our experience is that people are pretty elastic when you give them responsibility, and they just grow rapidly with the job."[2]

THE TEACHER

Indian managers respond well to one-on-one coaching from members of top management. The *guru–shishya* model of teaching and learning has deep roots in Indian culture, and the senior boss who takes on the role of a teacher exemplifies a venerated tradition. He or she gives selected subordinates personal coaching that is holistic, and not just about the nuts and bolts of work.

The subordinate, in turn, regards the lessons taught to him or her as unique because they can only be conveyed by someone who understands what it is like to be at the top. He or she develops a spectrum of abilities because the senior leader not only shows him or her the ropes of the business, but also provides direct advice on how to improve his or her managerial and leadership skills. The subordinate's confidence levels shoot up, and his or her relationship with this special superior is etched into his or her memories and remembered fondly years later.

Several of the executives who talked with us felt that they had been singled out and groomed by a superior. Here are two stories that illuminate this kind of special relationship.

Amardeep Learns to Say "No"

For Amardeep, learning to say "no" catapulted him from being a good manager to thinking like an executive. This lesson came to him from his immediate boss, Vikram Seth, vice president of manufacturing, who was only two years older than Amardeep. They had known each other for almost 10 years and Amardeep admired Vikram's ability to pinpoint the strengths and weaknesses of his subordinates. Vikram would then spend hours talking to his subordinates about themselves. "He really believed in developing the second line of leadership," said Amardeep. "So he identified a couple of people who were supposed to become future leaders in the company. There was one thing he told me. 'You are a good person, nice person,' he said. 'This is going to be your biggest enemy.'" Vikram went on to explain to Amardeep that once people call you a "nice" person, they develop expectations about how you will treat them. But a leader, by the very nature of his or her job, cannot always be a nice person, so others become angry with them. In turn, the leader becomes miserable, since he or she is not able to live up to his or her own image as a "nice person." This deep conversation galvanized Amardeep into learning to say "No." His talk with Vikram made him realize that despite his many fine qualities as a manager, this one deficit would block him from becoming a masterful senior executive.

Balachandran Is Spotted and Groomed

Balachandran had spent two years rotating among assignments on the shopfloor and in accounts, marketing, and sales. Then he was spotted by the president of the company, who selected him to be executive assistant for one year. Since the president was looking after two other companies in Delhi, he would visit the Kolkata company for about 10 days each month; and for the 20 days that he was in Delhi, Balachandran was responsible for going through all his correspondence. This was before the advent of email, and it was Balachandran's job to respond to all communications addressed to the president, whether by mail, phone, or fax. The president encouraged him to call with questions if necessary, but, for the most part, gave Balachandran minimal instructions.

"That was a fantastic training experience," said Balachandran, recalling gratefully how much he had learned. "I had a unique privilege. I am purposely calling it 'unique privilege.' He used to make me sit with him in any meeting that he would conduct. For 10 days, from the time he would enter his office in the morning until the time he left, I would be with him. He told me, 'Look, don't disturb me during the meeting, but you keep taking notes and if there is a question, something that you don't understand, make a note and after the meeting you can ask me and I will try and explain it to you.' Now, how many people can get this kind of coaching?" Today, Balachandran is the president of a subsidiary business in the automotive industry.

Not every manager will be selected and subjected to a strong mentor–protégé relationship. This does not mean that the opportunities to learn and grow are available to only a few. There are many different kinds of teaching–learning relationships, teachers can be found at all levels within an organization, and all teaching does not need to be at such a high level of intensity. Lessons too can come in different ways—as constructive advice, constructive feedback, a simple instruction, or even a painful reprimand:

- My boss said, "Don't give up on knowledge and every day, you must read for a while." Till today, I get up at 5.30 in the morning and read for an hour and half.

- He told me, "You are a very good worker but you are an awful communicator, and if this is how you are going to communicate, you will get nowhere in life. The fact is that you have to inspire confidence—by holding forth and by having the confidence to speak and hold the audience's attention. Make communication your strength and perfect your communication." And then he told me how.
- My manager walked into my office, sat opposite me and gave me a dressing down. It was one of those worst whiplashings I had ever received. He said, "Buddy, let me tell you something. You're so young. Your problem is your high energy. When you have a problem, what you do is you keep running around like a headless chicken."

This last manager admitted that even today, he sometimes starts running for the sake of running because he is uncertain about what to do. But his former boss's message still runs in his head; so he is not completely gripped by his earlier syndrome.

To summarize, teacher bosses are an important source of learning and help their subordinates to correct poor habits and form good habits. Some managers experience both the privileges and the obligations that go with being spotted and groomed by a senior leader. But this does not mean that managers who do not get personal teaching are hindered from advancement. Many superiors are willing to pass along what they themselves have learned through experience. They can be watched, or approached to share what they know about management and leadership; and when they provide powerful personal feedback, their subordinates can always use that valuable knowledge for self-improvement.

My views are woven through these pages: all managers can absorb learning—from the bosses they like and admire, and even from those whom they do not. This begs the question: what precisely are the central lessons to be learned from bosses? The stories in this chapter have already pointed to what bosses teach—consciously and unconsciously. The pointers are now made explicit as two important lessons that you, the future senior leader, can extract from your experiences with your bosses.

LESSON ONE: MANAGING AND MOTIVATING SUBORDINATES

How complicated can it be to motivate subordinates and get them to do their best work? The answer to that question is: much more complicated than most managers realize until they are promoted into their first supervisory assignment. As you take on the job of being a "good" boss, questions appear and easy solutions disappear. When you have the authority to tell employees what to do, why don't they automatically cooperate? How do you focus the attention of subordinates on the production goals that have to be met when their emotional energy is scattered across a variety of issues that they consider more important? What is to be done when a sales or marketing campaign does not go as planned and your dispirited team members begin to throw blame on each other for the failed initiative? Is firing an incompetent worker always the best solution? I think you get the point—when it comes to working with subordinates, a plethora of unforeseen questions come up. Managing and motivating others is difficult work.

At this juncture, you can reflect on what you have learned from your bosses and superiors up to now, and what you still need to learn. By working your way through the exercises that follow, you can create a plan of action for improving your skills of managing and motivating others.

Step 1: Pause and Reflect

This chapter has given you a vicarious experience of many different kinds of bosses. Do any of them remind you of someone you have known who left a mark on you? How so? Think back across all the bosses and superiors under whom you have worked. Who stands out in your memory? Why? How did this person or people contribute to your development as a leader and manager? Make a list of the most important lessons that you learned from them.

Now progress to thinking about whether you have applied any leadership lessons learned from various bosses. Can you give specific examples? Based on the thoughts that surface from this exercise, what are implications for how you behave as a boss? What example do you set for your subordinates? What are the leadership lessons you want to impart?

Step 2: Assess Yourself

The behaviors listed in table 2.1 are based on four decades of research concerning skills and perspectives that are necessary for effectively managing and motivating subordinates, and include the views of Indian executives. If you are already a boss, whether of one or many subordinates, you can use the assessment to evaluate yourself. If you are not a boss currently, recall a time when you were in charge of directing the work of others, perhaps in college or on a community project. Or imagine how you would behave if you were made a boss overnight. Using a scale of 1 to 5 (with 1 = Never, 2 = Occasionally, 3 = Often, 4 = Usually, and 5 = Always), give yourself a "frequency" rating. Honestly, how often do you follow these eight practices?

Step 3: Take Action

Next, you can plan a course of action. What are the practices for which you can give yourself a *shabash* ("well done") and where do you see the need for improving yourself? Select one or at most two practices that you want to adopt from now on. For example, perhaps you wish to *take an interest in the hopes and dreams of subordinates* and learn to *empower subordinates by*

Table 2.1 Assessment: Managing and motivating subordinates

Practice	*Self-rating*
Setting goals that energize the team	
Empowering subordinates by giving them responsibility, support, and trust	
Giving subordinates sufficient freedom to experiment	
Trusting that subordinates can learn to be competent	
Taking interest in the hopes and dreams of subordinates	
Recognizing and rewarding the contributions of others	
Assessing subordinates' strengths and limitations accurately	
Acting decisively and fairly when dealing with problem employees	

giving them responsibility, support and trust. Choose a couple of people whom you supervise, and with whom you wish to form a different kind of boss–subordinate relationship.

One way to show interest in your subordinates is to bring to mind people in your life who have taken an interest in you. These people could be former bosses or colleagues. Or they could be family members, former teachers, friends, or even strangers whom you met when traveling. What did they say and do to make you feel noticed? Slowly and sincerely, can you begin to show the same kind of interest in one or two of your subordinates?

Maybe none of your bosses has empowered you by giving you a challenging responsibility, voicing faith in your ability to get the job done, and encouraging you to come back for guidance or resources if you felt the need. If this is true, talk with others in your professional and personal circles to find out whether anyone has worked under a catalyst boss. Ask about the impact their catalyst boss had on them, and listen. Take from their stories the catalyst boss behaviors that feel natural to you. Try them on. Of course, in the beginning, any new behavior feels awkward. For example, for those who greet others with a *namaste*, shaking hands when being introduced to another may feel awkward. But as you persist in practicing different behaviors with subordinates, your new behaviors will slowly become habitual.

To summarize, the primary elements of your plan of action are: recollect what you may have experienced; or collect the experiences of others; then start on a small scale by selecting only one or two subordinates and practice one or two new ways of interacting with them. As you start to feel the difference in how they respond to you—perhaps with initial suspicion but with trust that increases over time—you will find yourself getting ready for the next lesson that is best imbibed from bosses and superiors.

LESSON TWO: DEVELOPING SUBORDINATES

Your approach to developing your subordinates will be intricately linked with the ways in which you manage and motivate subordinates. The formula is more easily said than done: to develop subordinates, bosses need to focus on them as people, and implement policies and practices that help them to learn and grow. Once again, the best approach is to take the three steps described in the previous section: pause and reflect, assess yourself, and take action.

Step 1: Pause and Reflect

Return to thinking about the bosses and superiors you have known. Did any of them point you toward a special developmental opportunity for which you owe them a debt of gratitude? Perhaps one of them took time out to talk about your career progress or personal development. If not a boss, some other person may have contributed to your development. Bring this relationship to the front of your mind, and then continue reading.

Table 2.2 Assessment: Developing subordinates

Practice	*Self-rating*
Providing useful and timely negative feedback	
Effectively delegating responsibilities	
Patiently coaching subordinates to help them handle difficult work	
Providing opportunities for subordinates to take on leadership roles	
Spotlighting subordinates' achievements to higher management	
Supporting initiatives that improve employee qualifications or competence	

Step 2: Assess Yourself

As earlier, using the scale of 1 to 5 (with 1 = Never, 2 = Occasionally, 3 = Often, 4 = Usually, and 5 = Always), give yourself an honest "frequency" rating. How often do you practice the six behaviors in table 2.2?

Step 3: Take Action

Repeating the process you followed earlier, select one or two practices that you wish to include in your repertoire of leadership behaviors. Has either of these behaviors been shown toward you? If yes, you can imitatively act in the same way with the one or two subordinates you select for this exercise. Ideally, your relationship with selected subordinates is such that you can inform them about your plan at some point, and ask them from time to time about whether they see any change in you. Whenever you are trying to behave differently, asking for feedback—directly from the people who are affected by your behavior—is one of the best ways of tracking your progress. Of course, this only works when there is mutual trust and respect.

IMPLICATIONS FOR INDIAN MANAGERS

As you progress on your path to becoming a better boss, remind yourself of this fact: when asked what experiences have shaped them into the leaders and managers that they are today, almost one-half of the top executives who were interviewed had a boss story to tell! In India, the boss and the superior's influence on shaping the leadership sensibilities of their subordinates are far more powerful than they sometimes realize. They are inevitably critically important developers of leadership talent. The variety and uniqueness of leadership lessons learned from superiors cannot be duplicated by other work experiences.

In the Indian business context, the boss–subordinate relationship is very special as it is considered akin to the *guru–shishya parampara* (teacher–student bond). The central feature of this symbiosis is *sneh–shradhaa*, the affection–devotion or deference between the teacher and the student. In Hinduism, *guru–shishya* relationships are founded on the genuineness of the guru and the humility, inquisitiveness, commitment, and obedience[3] of the student, because these are what lead to transformational learning. The relationship in and of itself is regarded as the best way to convey subtle, advanced knowledge, or *vidyā*.[4]

This chapter aims to help you form a variety of teaching–learning relationships. A point worth noting is that one, or even a few bosses, can seldom be the source of the many different leadership lessons needed to run today's complex organizations. Fortunately, bosses and superiors, both effective and ineffective, are everywhere. The judicious approach for emerging leaders is to observe and seek guidance from as many bosses and superiors as possible.

As underscored by the stories told, emerging leaders can always apply their powers of observation and reflection to form an image of the leader they want to be. From watchfulness, thoughtfulness, and conversations, they become discerning about what it means to be effective as a leader. For you, the implication is that this is the way to craft your distinctive style of leading and your personal leadership commitments.

In closing, here are the thought provoking words of J. R. D. Tata, a legendary thinker and doer, on what it meant to him to be a leader of people: "If I have any merit, it is getting along with individuals according to their ways and characteristics . . . At times it involves suppressing yourself. It is painful but necessary . . . to be a leader you have got to lead human beings with affection."[5]

ENDNOTES

1. *O Captain, My Captain*. Courtesy: www.tata.com. Available at http://www.domain-b.com/businessleaders/interviews/muthuraman_captain.htm.
2. S. Manallack, *Leadership Is Grooming Future Leaders* (2007). Available at http://www.dcmain-b.com/businessleaders/articles/20060930_grooming.htm.
3. D. Chakraborty & S. K. Chakraborty, *Leadership and Motivation: Cultural Comparisons* (New Delhi, India: Rupa & Co, 2006).
4. Global Oneness. Meaning of *Vidya*: A Wisdom Archive on Meaning of *Vidya*. Available at http://www.experiencefestival.com/meaning_of_vidya.
5. S. A. Sabavala, R. M. Lala, & J. R. D. Tata, *Keynote: Excerpts from His Speeches and Chairman's Statements to Shareholders* (New Delhi, India: Rupar & Co., 2004).

3

CREATING CHANGE—TAKING ON A TURNAROUND

Alam Kapur was running a manufacturing plant that had been accruing losses for its parent company, a large and highly competitive consumer goods conglomerate. With a huge workforce of 6,000 plus, the only way forward was to institute an early retirement program and start downsizing. This brought on regular confrontations with the union, and tensions between top managers and union leaders escalated. For the next two-and-a-half years, open hostility, the use of loud and abusive language, and successive strikes became normal. For Alam, stumbling with anxiety through each and every day was like "walking through a long tunnel, not knowing when it would end." But when the situation was finally brought under control by senior management, and the union leaders backed off, Alam realized that this experience was a turning point in his career. What he learned is that: "You have to go through a lot of these downsides. That's what gives you the strength and confidence to handle a variety of situations."

As in the case of Alam Kapur, being at the helm of creating change almost always imbues managers with confidence and awareness of personal strengths and limitations. Assignments to introduce change were a key source of personal development for two-thirds of all the top executives interviewed. Our analysis shows that change initiatives generate the greatest number and variety of leadership lessons (see table 1.1 and figure 1.2). Of all the essential leadership lessons that managers need to learn, almost a quarter ensue from "creating change" (see the appendix).[1]

The range of changes being introduced by Indian business leaders today is mindboggling, which means that there are many opportunities for young managers to participate in managing change. "Change" wears many guises, but broadly speaking, change-oriented assignments are either turnarounds or new initiatives (which will be discussed in the next chapter).

In this chapter, two kinds of turnarounds are described. The first is akin to a fix-it; the second involves shifting the culture of the entire organization. Scenarios and quotations reveal that managers implementing a turnaround go through intense waves of mixed and negative feelings. But the message from the narratives is clear—by creating change, managers become more confident and self-aware; and a turnaround specifically sharpens their execution skills. The point to note is that the Center's practical work of developing leaders over the past four decades has shown that two of the most crucial lessons in leadership are *confidence* and *self-awareness*; and managers who assume responsibility for leading change gain both. Furthermore, implementing a turnaround is the surest way to learn *effective execution*.

TURNAROUNDS OR FIX-ITS

Business turnarounds require fixing a failing or underperforming business operation. Sometimes, the financial performance of the business unit must be stabilized, often by restructuring or downsizing. At other times, problems left behind by previous managers must be tackled and resolved.

Turnaround situations are common to every industry—from agricultural research labs to banks and consumer goods outlets to manufacturing units. For the manager who is given a turnaround task, the goal of his or her assignment is to improve productivity and profitability. The growth of the business unit may have stalled, with the company incurring enormous losses due to market contraction. The financial and operational problems of the unit may have compounded because employees are deficient in skill, unwilling to perform, and pessimistic about the company's future, and distrust management. Difficulties with workforce skill levels and attitudes and the dilemmas of working with belligerent labor unions or political leaders are common.

The Herculean tasks that beset the manager accountable for the turnaround are captured by two descriptions that focus on their human reactions, not the details of their experience or learning. The reason for focusing on human reactions is that managers must first calm their turbulent thoughts and feelings and manage their anxiety about the circumstances in which they find themselves. Otherwise, it will be tough for them to learn any lessons in leadership. In the first scenario, the manager unwittingly walks into a business with serious operational issues. In the second scenario, the manager must improve the productivity of an under-resourced unit that has been sidelined by upper management. Here is what they said.

Cleaning Up a Mess

"I had just been appointed managing director of a medium-size company," said Mr. Khanna. "Within two weeks I realized I was sitting on a bomb. Nothing was right. The market conditions had deteriorated after September 11. The internet bubble had burst, the portfolio was poor, the company's financial reserves were exhausted, and the top team was simply not good enough. The expectations were huge, as the board thought they were sitting on a really great company. We had nothing—nothing, except the company brand."

Mr. Khanna realized that he was on his own, and had to figure out what to do without the support of others. His experience taught him "to be systematic about reshaping the destiny of a company without taking shortcuts."

Beating the Odds

"No investments were being made in our department because it was not the core business," commented Rajgopal.

> The equipment, and all that we had, were very old. We submitted many schemes, and people were sent abroad and came back and submitted more schemes. But the facilities would not come because we could not justify what we wanted, as far as a return on investment was concerned. Any time we asked for replacements, the management would not sanction that. We were saddened that we could not quickly increase our production or improve our lives. But we kept on working.
>
> Then we started examining our assumptions. Many things that we assumed to be right were not right. So much so that we ended up increasing our production and achieved a new record—without any investment, through a series of improvements—even though the equipment had become old.
>
> And then the learning! There is no one big improvement. It is not like there is a miracle cure or drug or formula. Improvements are a series of things. If you make five minor improvements, the ripple effect is a big improvement. If you are bent upon doing something, you will find the way. Resources are not the limitation, assumptions are.

As shown by these narratives, a feeling of fearsome responsibility hangs over the heads of managers accountable for remedying an underperforming or failing operation. But there are payoffs to them enduring immense tension. They become aware of their capabilities, realizing what they can and cannot do to "fix" the situation. For example, Mr. Khanna learned he could be self-reliant, visionary, systematic, and thorough. In the same way, just surviving pressures and solving complex problems increases confidence. For example, Rajgopal did not solve one problem as much as discover a way of generating solutions to problems—by examining limiting assumptions. Imagine what a boost this must have been to his confidence! Both managers also learned the art of getting the job done or executing effectively.

We turn next to descriptions of the second kind of turnaround: proactive, top-down efforts to alter the culture, systems, or structure of the business. This type of turnaround affects not just several units or functions, but the entire company.

TOP-DOWN TURNAROUNDS

Organizational turnarounds start with a deceptively simple official mandate necessitating an organizational culture change. Despite them having the authority to make change happen, delivering results is not at all easy for managers. For managers who roll out large-scale turnarounds, the job is a much bigger gamble than a business unit fix-it. Their success or failure is far more visible to everybody in their organization.

Widespread organizational changes are undertaken when the organization has to be repositioned in the market or the workforce must be persuaded to align around different priorities. Many Indian companies have been compelled to reorganize to become market driven, which is a departure from selling in a government-regulated environment. As the rollout moves forward, the rumblings of change are felt across the entire enterprise and at all levels.

Thorny issues arise: new offices and factories must be opened or surplus ones closed. Personnel have to be reassigned and the skills and attitudes of managers and employees have to be retooled almost overnight. Jobs must be redesigned. Some complications are typical. For example, managers with a technical or professional orientation resist becoming market oriented. Employees who have to adopt a new technology and reconfigure their work procedures are often reluctant learners.

The narratives that follow highlight, once again, the enormity of the manager's efforts and the intensity of the emotions that are stirred up inside them. Their assignment can shake them to their core, causing them to reflect deeply on their own human limitations and humanity. Alternately, some experience feelings of effectiveness and euphoria afterward. In the first narrative, the company was struggling financially and needed its people to believe that things could change and that their views mattered. In the second and third narratives, managers share their great sorrow at being obligated to make painful decisions.

Power of People, Power to People

Mr. Narayan learned to get widespread employee involvement to change the destiny of the company. He said:

> We were talking of thousands of people in the workforce and we were talking about multiple locations and we were talking about really having to create a completely different mindset. These were people who were very skeptical, with lots of doubts about the true intentions of top management. To get their confidence, we had to try and get them to believe that: "No, the management is concerned, the management is serious, the management actually wants to hear what you have to say and is willing to make commitments on the spot and then willing to get regular feedback."
>
> So there were a series of small presentations and lots of questions and answers to hear the voice of the customer, hear the voice of competitors in some cases, and get in farmers, get in labor union people, in a very frank and open discussion. Many times workers would stand up and really shout at me. I would, you know, either agree with them or not agree with them, with my full team sitting on the stage. Then at every table we would have a composition of workers, supervisors, officers, and very senior officers, all sitting at the same table, all sitting together and working on visioning or

> working on specific problems and creating solutions arising out of whatever strategy statements and details had been publicly shared. We would have 800 people in a *shamiana* (a large tent) working out detailed action plans and then signing off on them.

From implementing this large-scale interactive process, Mr. Narayan stumbled upon his passion for working with a large number of diverse people to arouse their motivation and energy and channel that toward a shared goal. The process itself was a peak experience for him, opening his eyes to his latent interests. He became aware of his own commitment to empower every kind of person—not just to rely on management graduates to come up with intellectual plans, but to work with people across the organization to craft and implement a shared intention.

Coping With Unendurable Circumstances

When the market is highly competitive, technologies are changing, and customers can take their business elsewhere, the only option is to restructure how the business operates. But the task is almost unendurable, especially when it involves layoff decisions.

"I couldn't share that with anybody, including my wife," confessed Mr. Mehra. "When I saw the names of my close friends and my relatives, I had to keep everything to myself. There was no one to talk to. What was going to happen? Who could I share that with? So emotionally it was very stressful . . . very stressful. I realized that with TQM, I could use logic. But here it was all the emotions."

To deal with his conflicting feelings, Mr. Mehra tapped into his own humanity. He could sense how the scars from this episode in the company's history would remain forever in the minds and hearts of those who had lost their jobs. He learned that although he had to implement a sorrowful course of action, he could do so without losing his personal connection with those who were affected.

Can Pain Bring Gain?

"Some businesses got divested and it was painful," said Mr. Chandrasekar, reflecting on how he had to decide whom to let go and how to inform them. His company was well known for valuing people, and most of the employees had grown with the company. But with share prices having nosedived, there was no other way, even though the company's reputation for its exemplary treatment of employees was at stake.

> You are not sacking—you are divesting a business. But can you redeploy all these people? It was my job to come out and say how I would identify the people to lay off. Some guy had worked there for 18 years . . . someone else had a daughter in college. These are things I had not experienced before. You do all you can as your part of due diligence. But at the end of the day, you have to put in your recommendation—"This is what we will do."

One lesson about executive responsibility became very evident to Mr. Chandrasekar: the executive has to own his decision. There was a great deal of ambiguity in the situation and it was never clear to him whether he was making the correct decisions. But he had to be able to think on his feet, work with others, and persuade them that in spite of the very difficult situation, the best decisions were being taken. "It was very painful. There were moments when I asked myself if someone would puncture the tires of the car I had parked downstairs. When I look back, I think that was the time when I grew up as a leader."

These detailed comments from executives who have implemented organizational turnarounds are rich sources of insight for those preparing to be senior leaders. They highlight that two of the main lessons learnt from turnarounds are *confidence* and the ability to *execute effectively*. We now examine these lessons in greater depth.

LESSON THREE: CONFIDENCE

Confidence is belief in oneself and a self-reliant or "can do" attitude. Confidence accrues from several different kinds of experiences. Surviving the stresses of severe job pressures and adversity is one. Solving problems is another. As described in later chapters, young Indian managers become more confident simply by speaking up in the presence of their bosses and superiors; and those who are singled out for recognition by an award, an appointment, or a promotion find that their confidence levels rise too.

Though managers' confidence levels can fluctuate, and reserves of confidence are high sometimes and low at other times, here are steps that you can take to increase your confidence.

Step 1: Pause and Reflect

What difficult situations have you dealt with in your life? The stories you have just read—for example about "cleaning up a mess" or "beating the odds"—may trigger your own recollections of a similar experience. Or perhaps you have undergone early life hardships or family problems that you have kept to yourself. An early or midlife job search may not have turned out as expected. If any of your experiences caused you to look inward, draw on your own inner resources to handle your situation, and become self-reliant, your level of self-confidence would have risen too.

Another question you can ask yourself is: "When have I solved a problem?" The size and nature of the problem are not relevant. For example, maybe you have helped a couple of colleagues to sort out their differences and start to work together amicably; or applied your technical skills to fixing a broken appliance or machine; or done market research that led to an increase in the sales of your company's products; or delivered a well-received presentation, where senior management took note of your recommendations.

What is relevant is how you handled the problem. The chances are that you responded instinctively—querying yourself about what was not working and figuring out what you could do. Your handling of the situation gave you a rush of feelings that validated that you are a capable person, that your actions make a difference, and that you are able to contribute to your colleagues or organization or community or family. These are the feelings of a confident person.

This reflective exercise entailing a review of incidents in your own life is meant to help you remind yourself that your efforts count. You are capable of producing results and remedies. The next step is to assess whether your behaviors show you to be a confident person.

Step 2: Assess Yourself

Using the scale of 1 to 5 (with 1 = Never, 2 = Occasionally, 3 = Often, 4 = Usually, and 5 = Always), rate yourself on the five behaviors in table 3.1. How often do you practice the behavior in each statement? As you respond, consider whether

Table 3.1 Assessment: Confidence

Behavior	*Self-rating*
Showing steadiness during difficult times	
Communicating confidently	
Speaking up in the presence of bosses and superiors	
Appreciating being singled out for recognition	
Managing job pressures without becoming overly tense	

your colleagues and friends would agree with the rating that you are giving yourself. Keeping this in mind, come up with your final ratings. This will give you a more accurate picture of whether you come across as confident.

Step 3: Take Action

For leaders, others' perceptions of them matter. You may feel confident inside yourself but not show that on the outside, or vice versa. If you are interested in demonstrating confidence, ask yourself this question: Which one behavior would you most want to change? Forming a goal is a good starting point for a plan for self-improvement.

For example, do you want to show steadiness during difficult times? If yes, find people who seem steady to you and ask them for their secret. Let yourself be inspired and resolve to emulate them. Maybe you want to speak up in the presence of superiors. Think about what may be some reasons for your holding back. Perhaps you have a background that is similar to Cyrus Rusheed's. Cyrus was in his mid-30s when he became aware that he hesitated to express his thoughts and ideas in front of superiors. But he was spontaneous and expressive with his peers. He began to think that it was a pity that he was shortchanging himself: unless he spoke up, no one would realize that he was a thorough and insightful thinker. With some introspection, he figured out that this habit was rooted in his childhood, when he had frequently been reminded to be quiet. His father was a writer who worked at home and required silence for hours on end. Cyrus was carrying over his childhood behavior into the workplace. Once he realized this, he chose to become less hierarchy ridden and to speak his mind, politely but firmly. He reminded himself that the worst that could happen would be that he would get into disagreements with others.

Whatever the new behavior you take on, give yourself at least three months of practice. Then ask someone with whom you work regularly, and whom you trust, whether they have noticed any changes in you.

LESSON FOUR: EFFECTIVE EXECUTION

Managers who know how to execute a plan command respect—because when any kind of change has to be introduced, execution is what counts. Executing effectively is having the skills to get the job done and knowing many tactics for working with people to achieve results. The managing director of a consumer goods manufacturing company advised: "Don't worry. Just go ahead, keep going ahead, and get it done. This is the whole thing about 'bias for action'—just getting the job done. The fact that you get it done also gives you a lot of satisfaction." His comments point out that executing effectively is its own reward because it brings self-satisfaction. After all, the paramount task of a leader is to work with others to achieve satisfying results.

For almost one-third of the interviewed senior executives, the know-how for getting results is a critically important lesson learned from turnaround assignments. A complex turnaround begs to be broken into a series of smaller projects, so that a huge undertaking can come to fruition. Therefore, project management work, with its imperative to meet targets and deadlines, pushes managers to become skilful at execution. Very simply, the prescription for achieving results, or effective execution, is to pay persistent attention to operational details and to people.

Step 1: Pause and Reflect

Have you sought out or been given the opportunity to manage projects? Were you able to get feedback on whether you performed competently as a project manager? Did your organization or boss encourage you to attend project management training or did you seek advice from others to improve your skills?

Execution skills are not usually taught in business schools, management development programs, or executive education courses. So it is all the more important for you to create experiences for yourself that necessitate attention to logistical and operational details and relationships with people. In this way, you will lay the foundation for taking on the arduous work of creating change in your organization at a later stage in your career. As your execution skills sharpen—by your engagement with fix-its, turnarounds, and organizational change work—success will become more likely. Success builds on success; so your subsequent, more complex endeavors will further hone your executive ability. The self-assessment in step 2 can help you to identify which skills and behaviors you need to fine tune.

Step 2: Assess Yourself

Using the scale of 1 to 5 (with 1 = Never, 2 = Occasionally, 3 = Often, 4 = Usually, and 5 = Always), rate yourself on the behaviors in table 3.2. How often do you practice the behavior in each statement? As you respond, consider whether your boss would agree with the rating that you are giving yourself. If you think that there will be a discrepancy between the self and boss ratings, ask yourself why this is so. Adjust your ratings so that they portray your skills realistically.

Step 3: Take Action

Previous sections on how you can "take action" have offered general guidance. This is because a book can provide only broad principles, not specific instructions, on how you can develop yourself or cultivate productive relationships. You and your relationships are uniquely configured, so a formulaic solution to your particular developmental needs is not possible.

Table 3.2 Assessment: Effective execution

Behavior	*Self-rating*
Attending to details when implementing a plan	
Organizing work to meet deadlines	
Monitoring subordinates performance when needed	
Controlling costs to maintain or achieve profitability	
Devising practical solutions to operational problems	
Meeting important goals by delegating accountability as necessary	
Effectively coordinating people, budgets and other resources to deliver results	
Creating a common vision when initiating complex changes	
Recognizing that changes have an emotional impact on people	

But when it comes to executing projects (as a basis for creating change), specific tips can help you to succeed. The two prescriptions that follow are for managing projects effectively. They have been distilled from their own experiences by executives who have made it to the top.

A. Pay attention to details. This means being watchful about how plans and guidelines are implemented and using metrics carefully. These words of advice are worth heeding:

- "At the end of it, as an individual, what I learned is that the devil is in the details." (Managing director, IT division)
- "There may be broad guidelines, but the manner in which they are interpreted for a specific unit has to be specific. Guidelines cannot be applied blindly. If there is no independent verification of what is really happening at the ground level, there will be an abuse of guidelines, and much will be brushed under the carpet." (Executive vice president, corporate strategy)

- "You need to be constantly on the guard, constantly looking out for process improvements. What is important for me is actively looking for areas where you believe that there could be a possibility of things going wrong. What I actually learned, and I am trying to practice, is that small signals about things going wrong should never be ignored." (Senior general manager, structured finance group)
- "Many times, 'measurement' was not existing. For example, was the truck a 12- or 15-ton truck? We did not know. From no measurement, we went to measurement. That is definitely a basic improvement to operations. So this is when you start getting lots of results." (General manager, operational excellence)

B. Pay attention to people. Balancing their counsel to keep a close watch on implementation details, the executives offered equally strong advice to keep a close eye on people. Often, in work settings in India, the employees' skill levels have to be monitored and deficits have to be removed. According to one savvy general manager, there is typically a 20/80 equation, with 20 percent of subordinates showing huge amounts of perseverance and 80 percent needing close follow-up for the job is to be executed to specifications. This and similar pragmatic perspectives are reflected in these comments.

- "We realized that people don't perform because they don't know enough. So we went on to train every operator, including the person who was sweeping the floor. And after the training session was over, I would cross-check with the operator whether he had understood. And we actually had to repeat this exercise seven times on an average, before everybody understood Total Quality Responsibility." (Managing director, consumer goods company)
- "The concept of deskilling the job is to make sure you break up everything into its simplest parts so that anybody

can actually do it and so that you end up with hundreds of noncomplex operations. At the same time, invest very heavily into the training and development of people. We are then able to run with enormous amounts of complexity without necessarily becoming overwhelmed by the complexity. This approach has been extremely successful."

- "Every new management trainee is made to go through these procedures, which are often revised through experience. Learning has to be documented and put into procedures. And then others are taught and trained and all of this information is on the intranet." (Divisional CEO, hotels)

The advice from the executives (concerning operational details and people) is straightforward: develop procedures, document procedures, revise procedures; then train, train, and train once again.

The main way for you to prepare yourself for very complicated assignments that will occur later in your career is by managing projects. So I conclude with a story that synthesizes the main points about how project management experience develops the skills of effective execution, which is a key ingredient in a leader's recipe for delivering results.

Early in his career, Mr. Chattopadhay was given the responsibility of staging a national agro-industry exhibition and fair that would be attended by chief ministers from five states. To achieve this, he had to supervise 40 professionals, coordinate with half-a-dozen government departments, and involve various state governments and private agencies. His responsibilities involved all aspects, from fundraising to setting the entrance fees to finding and contracting with the exhibitors. Chattopadhay had to work night and day because there were so many things pending and the deadlines had to be met—everything had to be completed in two months for the scheduled and highly publicized inauguration.

As he worked, Mr. Chattopadhay became aware of his talent and ability to work with different kinds of people, whether they were senior secretaries and bureaucrats who were coming to the fair or contractors with whom he had to negotiate. There were crises that had to be managed too. A tent collapsed, and the man caught underneath died. Later in the project, a fire broke out but was brought under control.

An unexpected complication was that Mr. Chattopadhay had to resolve tensions with a general manager of a local factory whose ideas about how to stage the national fair and exhibition were different from his. This general manager would give independent directives to Mr. Chattopadhay's team, thus creating conflicts. "The fellow would come and start creating some kind of fight. I had to immediately intervene and explain to these other people to keep their tempers low. I used to manage the situation so that it didn't really go out of control. From head office, they had told me very clearly, 'You can run the whole show. But see that this person is also not hurt.'" Ultimately, by having many, many conversations with both this general manager and his own team, Mr. Chattopadhay was able to manage conflicts and not let tempers flare out of control.

Project management calls for an uncompromising focus on deliverables and deadlines. Mr. Chattopadhay explained how the single most important lesson he learned was to not lose sight of the goals and objectives that had been set for him. "It was a tremendous opportunity for me to do this fair successfully in two months. I had never done these kinds of things in the past," he said, "and it was really a very big challenge. It increased my confidence that I could handle any responsibility that was thrust upon me."

IMPLICATIONS FOR INDIAN MANAGERS

For a manager in today's rapidly evolving and predatory business environment, creating and implementing change are necessary and inevitable. The opportunities to create change are plentiful, and as you progress on your pathway to senior leadership, seizing these opportunities is vital. Not only do you showcase your talents, you also feel the boost to your confidence, self-awareness, and execution ability. As indicated by an overwhelming majority of leaders, change initiatives teach the most comprehensive and practical lessons in leadership. They offer a unique, experience-based, up-to-date leadership curriculum that is relevant to the business environment in which managers currently operate.

Change, though imperative, is painful. References to the "trials and tribulations" endured by managers on a turnaround assignment have threaded through this chapter. Change means destroying the old to give way to the new, and preparing oneself for the mental and emotional anguish this brings. So it is worth recalling one fundamental principle within the Indian philosophical tradition. This principle manifests in the worship of the divine trinity: Brahma the Creator, Vishnu the Preserver, and Shiva the Destroyer.[2] Indian wisdom traditions acknowledge and celebrate change as a cycle of creation, sustenance, and destruction that is everlasting. This cyclical view of change is a source of the reservoirs of resilience that Indian managers can draw on to endure the difficulties intertwined with change.

ENDNOTES

1. Appendix, figure A.2.
2. V. Jayaram, *Introduction to Hindu Trinity*. Available at http://www.hinduwebsite.com/hinduism/hindutrinity.asp.

4

CREATING CHANGE—LAUNCHING A NEW INITIATIVE

> I have the confidence that I can start afresh and rebuild anything. As long as we have been given a running organization, and we have been running it, we don't know what we can create. One of the biggest benefits I have now, due to the experience of the past six years, is that I know that I can create . . . not just inherit, not just manage, but create. I have started and kicked off many businesses [at the bank]. Today I can say, "Okay, if I want, I can join a new organization and do something afresh."
>
> —*Executive director, retail banking group*

The stories in this chapter are from Indian business leaders who have launched one or more initiatives. The confidence and self-awareness in the voice of this executive director are echoed in comments from other top leaders. Their feelings of excitement and satisfaction come through repeatedly. Their remarks shine with the pride of creating something new and achieving something special:

- The entire experience was rather exhilarating because you feel that you are actually creating something new.
- There again, for me to be able to apply my mind to a totally new situation—new situation for the country, for my company, and for myself—and earn the respect of all the participants of

the system—the client, other investors, my own company, and my team, which is learning on the assignment along with me—that was, you know, a remarkable experience.

- I was handpicked by our chairman, and he entrusted me with the responsibility of starting this new business. That was in fact one of the most significant events of my career because this was a completely new opportunity. To start a new business from scratch—it required all my skills, all my inner capabilities.

New initiatives are welcomed because they signal the onset of favorable business conditions. The organization responds proactively to the prospect of rapid growth, either within or outside India or both. Senior leaders make plans to establish their company's clout among other domestic and international businesses. Multiple plans are laid, and many projects and exploratory ventures are kicked off. The responsibilities shouldered by the company's managers are exhilarating and full of satisfying new learning.

Opportunities to create changes in Indian business organizations are currently plentiful, and we gathered numerous stories. As the stories show, many lessons are learned from new initiatives: how to be innovative and entrepreneurial, navigate politics and gain influence, improve expertise in many domains, and gain confidence and self-awareness. Turnaround assignments and new initiatives both create change. But ending something old, as in a turnaround or fix-it, brings stress from apprehension, sorrow, and other unconstructive feelings; while starting something new brings stress that is invigorating.

NEW INITIATIVES

A new initiative is an opportunity to develop or launch new products and services, adopt new technologies, craft a new policy or process, build a plant or unit from scratch in another region or country, or embark upon a new line of business. Unique to this assignment is the manager's sense that he or she is starting with a tabula rasa and can create something novel and useful that has not existed before. Of course, this is not a one-person show. As the original idea and implementation unfold, the project draws on the ideas, enthusiasm, and labor of a multitude of other people. The process of exploring, planning, and launching the initiative starts waves that affect many people and processes. In small or big ways, new initiatives redirect the business purpose of the organization.

The diversity of possibilities is limitless, since the shape and direction of the change are constrained only by the imagination, ambition, and tenacity of the change maker or makers. Illustrations of the many forms a new initiative can take include:

- startups—such as opening up a new branch for a bank, or a sales office in a new country, or a new factory or greenfield unit, or a subsidiary of a foreign multinational
- new products and brands—for example, a new product that diversifies the company's line of products, or a marketing campaign that creates a brand and brand loyalty
- new services or a new service concept—such as corporate or personal financing schemes, debt servicing processes, or distribution systems that serve rural populations
- new joint ventures and collaborations—such as public–private sector partnerships or supply chain development based on international sourcing
- new policy development followed by legislation—for example, bank loans for the SME sector, or legislation introduced to open up the agrobusiness industry
- new market entry—such as by customizing products for domestic markets or developing brands for foreign markets

- new technology applications—for example, programs for the internet-based screening of job applicants, computerized payroll, or e-commerce ventures.

These examples skim the surface of the vast and rich possibilities that are yet to be imagined. Perhaps that last statement sounds exaggerated. It is not, as will become evident through the five case examples that follow. By all accounts, new initiatives start with a seemingly risky or wild idea. The groundwork involves dozens of conversations with many people from within and outside the organization. Improvisation, experimentation, and mistakes follow—but the team perseveres, sometimes over years. New knowledge and expertise are picked up along the way. The implementation process gradually gathers momentum and then takes off. A breakthrough is achieved—and after that, to maintain momentum, more people and resources are needed than originally foreseen. The impact of the initiative becomes broad and deep, moving in directions that are different from the original plan. In the process of creating change, the managers themselves are changed, transforming to become more confident and self-aware.

The five case examples are sequenced from the least to most complicated, relative to the scope of the original endeavor. The first episode shows off Shakander Singh's pride in his prowess, tracing how he goes into an unfamiliar sales territory, starts an office from scratch, builds his organization's customer base, and then basks in the recognition he gets from headquarters.

The Man from the North Succeeds in the South

With only three years of experience at marketing pesticides, Shakander Singh relocated from Punjab to Tamil Nadu as regional sales manager. He lacked knowledge of the region, its people and culture, and could not speak a word of Tamil. He was succeeding a senior manager who had come up through the ranks, worked in the region for more than 20 years, and knew the market like the back of his hand. Soon after Shakander's move, due to further decentralization of the sales function, he was charged with selecting the site for a new office, putting in its systems, hiring the first few employees, staging the inauguration, and building the business.

The memory that Shakander still cherishes from that personally momentous inauguration day are the words of his CEO as they went up in the lift after the event: "[Moving to Tamil Nadu] is the best decision you have taken because it will give you a lot of confidence in dealing with diverse people and cultures." Shakander felt that the CEO's words shaped his view of himself and what he had to do.

This is what Shakander actually did. For the first four months, he traveled incessantly to meet every customer several times over. His language disability turned into an advantage. His customers were hugely entertained by a Punjabi's fumbling attempts to speak Tamil. Meanwhile, business communications in broken English worked just fine. What Shakander learned was that his technical expertise (which was a given) did not matter as much as his ability to relate to his team and make sound business decisions. His team included many senior managers, but they responded well to him because he was objective, transparent, and fair in terms of what he expected from each of them.

Shakander's biggest asset was fearless decision making, particularly because timely decisions are critical in agriculture-based seasonal markets. "In business, you are always making decisions," he said. "Sell or not sell. Sell today or sell tomorrow. How much to sell and how much to hold. I was never fearful of handling commercial decisions and projections. At one level, a lot of young managers want more authority. At another level, they are very fearful of making decisions because their decisions may be right or may be wrong." He went on to describe how all decisions concerning the timely sales of seasonal products have immediate and visible monetary implications, which intimidates young managers.

Shakander's skills at managing an increasingly large sales team and growing the volume of business over a three-year period were noticed. He was asked to take over the mismanaged northeastern region and promoted. He went on to a fix-it experience from which he learned other important leadership lessons.

The next episode describes how Mr. Ali forged a partnership between his bank and the local municipal government to underwrite a housing development scheme. The relationship itself is a first, and spawns several other successful commercial ventures for his bank.

The Public-Private Sector Partnership that Launched a Housing Scheme

Salman Ali's privatized bank had posted him as branch manager to a city in northwestern India. Upon Salman's arrival, Mr. Patnaik, the chief executive of the municipal development authority, solicited his help for underwriting a housing scheme. "*Bhai*, we will give you business provided you help me," he offered. Mr. Patnaik then described his predicament. He felt sure that if he turned over the project to his own municipal management team, the initiative would bog down in bureaucratic procedures and deal making. "I want you to formulate the scheme, float the scheme, and do whatever you want for advertising." However, he told Mr. Ali not to expect any resources, though perhaps nominal supplements could be arranged.

Seeing a business opportunity, Salman asked himself, "Why not?" and became 100 percent committed to do the needful. He collected inputs from the municipal officers, figuring out the scope of the region to cover, the customer base to target, and many details. He took charge of putting together a booklet that used the just-introduced screen-printing technology. Salman took full advantage of the free publicity to market his bank's other products and services on the front, back, and inside covers. The booklet was sold at a small profit in all the branches of the bank, with proceeds used to advertise the housing scheme in leading newspapers. The bank later used Salman's booklet as a prototype to promote similar schemes across the country.

This first project was so successful that the municipality engaged Salman's bank to promote several other initiatives. Mr. Ali reflected on how this assignment was a turning point in his career because of how the banking operations were coupled with marketing. The strength of their relationship with the municipality became trend setting, and an extension counter of the bank was subsequently opened in the municipal offices.

Mr. Ali felt that though he was instrumental in getting the work done, he "was held by the people and the team that did the work." He acknowledged that the episode was a landmark for the bank and for him, and gave him a lot of satisfaction.

The third episode sees Ajay and his boss take on an entrepreneurial venture—from forming an idea about manufacturing and selling nationally branded garments in the Indian market to securing the funding, putting up the factories, and securely establishing a high sales volume.

The Business Model that Worked

Why not use the cost efficiencies of standardized factory production to turn out unique, Indian-branded garments for Indians? And why not pump up an existing sales volume of 1,000-to-2,000 to 100,000 clothing units a month? Ajay and his boss Vijay had started to dream big dreams. They wanted their high-end fashion garments to have a Rs. 1,000 look and feel, but carry an affordable Rs. 299 price tag.

They had to be inventive to glamorize the nationwide brand, uniquely customize garments, and keep production costs low. The notion that appealed to them was to franchise two processes: manufacturing the cloth and stitching customized garments. The popular movie star Akshay Kumar had already introduced the concept of branded cloth—two meters (2.2 yards) of material that consumers would purchase and then have their tailors customize into a garment of their choosing. Pepsi's model for softdrink distribution gave them yet another distribution model to think about. Starting with these ideas, they worked out the details of their own franchising model.

To cut transportation costs, they toyed with the idea of putting the textile manufacturing factories close to the end-purchaser. Soon the idea of setting up 12 textile manufacturing plants around the country took hold. Then, to customize garments, they considered having the garments stitched at the point of purchase. "Sindhis are built differently from Andhra Pradeshis, and Punjabis from Bengalis, and people from each region have distinctive fashion preferences anyway," they reasoned. So they opted to co-locate locally recruited tailors within the factory.

All that remained was to put their plan into action! That work fell to Ajay, who learned much about himself in the process. "This bit about going into an uncertain environment, trying to make different pitches—this is what gives me a kick," he admitted. Ajay "ran around the country," getting the machinery and the people into place. He found investors and sold them on the project. As he experienced setting up factories 12 times over, he realized how much he loved the adventure of creating something out of nothing and that he had the knack of doing so. Ajay credited his successes to his visionary boss "whose passion used to speak for itself." Of this boss, Ajay said: "He gives you the entire responsibility, so you tend to take the entire responsibility."

The fourth episode captures what is necessary for a large conglomerate to learn to originate many new lines of business. The narrative focuses on a small part of the action on one initiative—the manufacturing and sales of safety matches.

What's in a Safety Match?

Senior management had resolved to use their core business as a platform to spin off several subsidiary businesses. The matchmaking business was just one of several new ventures that were proposed. Mr. Kheriya's story about how his company learned to clone itself into new businesses is compelling. This is because the learning is not about how an established company can start one new venture, but about how that company can start any new venture.

Due to the parent company's experience with new ventures, the new-business launch cycle time had come down from nine to five months. At the outset, Mr. Kheriya told his people: "We do not have the clout of an elephant or the power of a lion. But we need the flexibility of a deer to step across this difficult terrain." His message took hold: the team set a new record of four months between kicking off the idea and putting safety matches into the market.

Mr. Kheriya started by borrowing key senior, middle, and junior managers from their core business. Of course, the core business still had to be managed effectively, so as not to collapse. Plus the "borrowed" managers had to be assured that they would not lose their jobs and positions in the core business. The trick was to create small teams, give them extensive autonomy, and set up multiple lines of communication that were short and fast. The team was charged with being bottom line oriented from day one.

"This was satisfaction of a different order," commented Mr. Kheriya. "Spinning out a new business from the family fold was like letting a little bird take off and fly off on its own." The practice of borrowing managers from the core business to start up other lines of business worked well for the company. So did the parameters they established: small autonomous teams; access to others for quick, multiple communications; and a meet-the-bottom-line directive. Each of their spinoffs turned into a profitable business. The safety matches flourished to such an extent that a few years later, the company bought out their primary foreign competitor in India.

The fifth and final episode shows how a small idea, born in a day-long conversation between two restless and creative minds, became an independent force that transformed the lives of Indian villagers.

Innovation Multiplied: One-Stop Shops in Rural India

Kumarji was ready to challenge himself. He wanted to stretch, to make mistakes and recover, and to learn. At that point, Kumarji was heading up one among a big group of companies in agrobusiness. He and his team had successfully navigated several internal business mergers, grown a larger portfolio of agricultural products, and developed an export capability. But the company was on a plateau. The parent company could not invest in future growth due to costs and risk factors; and the option of selling off the business below market value did not make sense.

Kumarji seriously considered moving to another company, and stopped to talk with his chairman. Their early morning discussion lasted through the day and into the evening because the conversation took a different direction. E-commerce ventures were mushrooming, Amazon had just come into the book market space, digital technologies were taking off, and the internet boom was at its peak. Although agricultural products had to be physically produced, transported, and consumed, the chairman challenged Kumarji to go back to the drawing board and look at business models in other industries and geographies. Why not harvest the decades of collective experience of their seasoned management team to come up with a different business model?

Kumarji buried himself in reading widely and in holding a series of brainstorming sessions at the divisional level. Initially, everywhere they looked, they saw constraints. The Indian small-farmer economy was regulated locally by *mandis*. All wholesale transactions occurred within the four walls of the *mandi*, where the farmer had no option but to accept the auction value of his produce, which would spoil quickly if not sold. Nor were the agricultural products guaranteed to be of consistently high quality. To sum up, the agrobusiness landscape was dotted with small-scale farmers operating with little information and limited concern for quality, and under draconian government regulations.

Slowly, the collective perspective of the group started to change. Why not think of their company as a service rather than a commodity business? The team began to place the spirit of customer service at the center of their thought process. They included the higher quality requirements of international grain distributors in their thinking.

This meant that they had to look at their supply chain differently. From the re-look, many next steps emerged. For example, though it took several years, the company worked on new legislation to update the archaic 40-year old Agricultural Produce Marketing Act. It conceived of putting internet technology in villages to give the farmers access to competitive pricing information. Although the team had started by reorganizing their supply chain to improve company competitiveness, they found themselves improving the competitiveness of the illiterate farmers. Until then, the farmers had not seen computers and only minimally listened to radio broadcasts for information about their market environment. But that was about to change.

Improving company competitiveness evolved into a far more passionate commitment to improving the quality of life of India's rural poor. For all levels of managers engaged in the initiative, there was an unexpected alignment of a broad social agenda with organizational goals and individual passions. As the saying goes, one thing led to another, putting into motion the co-evolution of sustainable innovation. This is the chain of events that occurred.

First the company had to move into providing satellite installations to get teleservices up and running. The installations were manned by a *sanchalak*—the lead farmer who maintained the computing facility in his home and made it accessible to other farmers from several neighboring villages. The *sanchalak*'s home office evolved into a one-stop shop that included health and education facilities, fuel stations, and a food court. This became the beginning of a rural retail business, or *choupal* or e-Choupal (as it came to be known). Soon it became apparent that the e-Choupal afforded an opportunity for the company to sell its related products. So the *sanchalak*'s role became that of a part-time company representative, and the e-Choupal became a full-scale retail outlet for the villages in the vicinity.

How and why did this happen? The company representatives responsible for setting up the *sanchalak*'s home office were treated with great courtesy by the villagers and plied with food and, of course, *chai*. The reps were embarrassed because they were not reciprocating the villagers' hospitality. They asked their bosses about setting up reception areas where the villagers could sit while waiting to access the computer. A natural follow-on was to make other amenities available to the villagers, who had journeyed long distances to get pricing information. They were all enacting the strongly valued Indian tradition of reciprocity and hospitality toward strangers. The concept of e-Choupals, or hypermarkets, formed itself during the interactions among people in the reception area. E-Choupals became a trendsetting innovation in India's rural life. Today, 6,500 *sanchalak*-operated e-Choupals are up and running, and serve 40,000 villages and 4 million farmers.[1]

By making consumer need central to their thinking, company representatives and villagers co-evolved a pioneering format for rural retail business. With top managers infusing the value of "service to rural Indians," senior managers contributing strategic thinking, middle managers providing coordination, and junior managers taking on execution, the whole new concept of community-based innovation came into existence. The villagers became the idea generators. Junior and midlevel managers became experimenters, testing feasibility and de-risking the business operations. Senior management surveyed the results of many tested business experiments and looked across sites to uncover which experiments merited investment for business growth. Top management took responsibility for finding the funding to drive this bottom-up, resource-intensive innovation machine.

This case demonstrates the far-reaching impact of a new initiative on not just individual managers or their team or organization, but the rural populations in several states.

CULLING THE LESSONS LEARNED

These stories may have triggered your memories of a new initiative in which you participated—small, medium, or large in scope. By reliving and reframing your experience, you can tap into a wealth of information, ideas, and inspiration. New initiatives are an extraordinary source of learning. A holistic review of your thoughts, feelings, and actions from different angles, as described in the following, will yield rich insights.

Step 1: A Holistic "Pause and Reflect"

If you can start by convening a few colleagues who are willing to travel back in time to uncover their own experiences with launching new initiatives, so much the better. By taking turns to tell stories, looking at the stories from multiple perspectives, asking clarifying questions, and mulling over the leadership lessons that were learned, your colleagues and you will broaden your insights about creating forward-looking change.

These questions, which each person can answer, are a good starting point. What was the opportunity? What was the assignment meant to achieve? What was the role that the narrator and others played? How did the initiative evolve over time and what were the outcomes that were ultimately reached?

The next set of questions stimulates a deeper look at how individuals were affected by their experience, with each person's contribution based on the initiative they just described. What was surprising about the way the assignment played out? Did the circumstances create stresses for them and how did those manifest? Bringing to mind their thoughts and feelings before, during, and after the assignment, what kind of a journey was the assignment? For example, if asked to give a headline about the experience for a magazine or for a newspaper article in the Sunday magazine section, what would the narrator say?

In the final round, the story narrators contribute their thoughts on the most important lessons in leadership they learned. The group makes note of the common and the unique themes emerging from what is said. This highlights relevant insights for future use. The discussion closes with reflections on whether and how each person applied their learning.

This comprehensive review of your own and others' experiences is a first step. The next steps are to assess yourself and take action so that you become more *self-aware*; better understand how to be *innovative and entrepreneurial*; and improve your skills at *navigating politics and gaining influence*. (Of the two other lessons imparted by new initiatives, *confidence* has been discussed in chapter 2 and *functional and technical expertise* will be discussed in chapter 7.)

LESSON FIVE: SELF-AWARENESS

Self-awareness is grounded self-knowledge. Many of us think we know ourselves since we are with ourselves all day, each day. But self-knowledge about abilities, limitations, emotional needs, and values is astonishingly difficult to acquire. Part of self-awareness is sensing our impact on others, which is even trickier to grasp. Whether we are seven or 70 years old, fresh self-insights continually a rise from us encountering new people and events. Our reactions reveal information about ourselves that we did not have before. Through the years, self-awareness continues to unfold, as executives acquire an intimate working knowledge of themselves.

A caveat: "self-awareness" is slippery to assess. We are a mystery to ourselves, and do not know how much we do not know. From a behavioral perspective, there are no objective anchor points to inform us about the gap between current and desired levels of self-awareness. Since it makes little sense to ask readers to pause and reflect on what they do *not* know about themselves, I provide an assessment for you to appraise your habitual behaviors for gaining self-awareness. These behaviors have been identified by the CCL professionals from four decades of experience with leadership development programs. The behaviors, if practiced diligently, become habits that improve self-awareness.

Step 2: Assess Yourself

Using the scale of 1 to 5 (with 1 = Never, 2 = Occasionally, 3 = Often, 4 = Usually, and 5 = Always), rate yourself honestly on how often you practice the four behaviors in table 4.1.

Step 3: Take Action

To guide you to develop a plan of action, three indicators of self-awareness are described. These indicators help you to

Table 4.1 Assessment: Self-awareness

Behavior	*Self-rating*
Seeking feedback from others	
Handling criticism effectively	
Observing the impact on others of my words and actions	
Admitting personal mistakes	

monitor the shifts in your personality, which are originating in your increased self-awareness. As described next, the shifts are in your perspectives on yourself; your relationships; and the purpose of your work.

A. Perspective on self. Hidden talents are discovered. This revolves around an "Aha!" about a newly found ability that you enjoy using—such as taking risks, making charismatic presentations, or facilitating idea generation in large groups. For example, in our interviews, Maya Sirkar discovered her zest for being an entrepreneur when she was asked to apply the concept of structured finance to a Rs. 1,000 crore loan to a leading Indian conglomerate (a crore is 10 million or 100 lakh). Over a period of nine months, she worked with multiple individuals within and outside her company to review the business opportunity from novel angles, change her thinking quickly and decisively, and develop new product solutions. Arjun Khosla's midcareer opportunity to teach MBA students at a prestigious Indian Institute of Management brought his gift for teaching to the fore; he found out that students gave his courses the highest ratings.

B. Perspective on co-workers. One's own superior or self-limiting attitudes toward co-workers surface, and precipitate a change in behavior. Ajay Gupta saw that his impatient and dismissive attitude toward those who did not grasp accounting fundamentals easily had set him on a lonely path; his colleagues simply did not want to work with him. Vikram Duvedi felt embarrassed when he discovered his deep-seated disrespect for long-time employees without an academic credential. Ram Bhatia wondered why he overtrusted others when the news that one of his subordinates was guilty of serious financial mismanagement became public. Each of these managers changed. Ajay taught himself patience. Vikram realized that although his senior co-workers were not ambitious, upwardly mobile fast trackers, many were involved in leadership activities in their own communities in education, social welfare, professional organizations, and their family and friendship circles. He began to value that their goals in life were different from his, and related to them with newfound respect. After chastising himself for his naiveté about people, Ram resolved to observe others more closely and understand their motivations more accurately. The changed attitudes and behaviors of all three managers created more effective working relationships for them.

C. Perspective on work. The personal meaning of work is discovered and affirmed. R. Subramaniam concluded that his belief in the value of his work and sense of personal responsibility were central to his work commitment; this gave him equanimity during easy and difficult times. When Anupam Thite took charge of a completely mismanaged branch of a national bank, and set about changing employee attitudes, developing documentation procedures, and much else, he experienced his first rush of success. That is when he recognized that for him, work was not about marking time but surmounting obstacles to achieve results. Given the chance to become a senior manager at an internationally branded telecommunications company, G. Thakur walked away from the high salary and secure job. He was determined to follow his heart into a line of work involving mechanical or electrical, but not electronic, engineering.

To synthesize, the main elements of your action plan are simply to pay more attention to your self, that is, your talents and preferences; how you relate with others and your impact on them; and why your work is important to you.

LESSON SIX: INNOVATION AND ENTREPRENEURSHIP

The questions worth asking yourself are: are you willing to use nontraditional ways of solving problems, experiment, tolerate mistakes that you and others will make, and take the risk that you may fail and not meet your objectives? Your responses are a clue about how similar your mindset is to that of managers who instinctively bring fresh perspectives to situations and find new solutions to problems. The attitudes and actions common to managers of this ilk are illustrated by the themes that thread through the five case examples in this chapter. In all the stories, the storytelling executives were willing to:

- interact closely and repeatedly with people from a variety of backgrounds and levels
- take bold but prudent risks, and do business in ways that had not been attempted before
- maintain a laser-like focus on achieving business results.

Step 1: Stop and Reflect

Perhaps you already think of yourself as innovative and entrepreneurial. If so, think about what has contributed to your own past successes, making notes for your personal use. A tried-and-true way to achieve success in any activity is to continue to repeat patterns of thought and behavior that have worked and discontinue patterns that have not.

Maybe you want to become more innovative and entrepreneurial. One way to start is by reviewing the five stories to search for actions that you can see yourself imitating. Then make notes about initiatives that you can attempt. Having thought through your own commitment to becoming innovative and entrepreneurial, you can assess yourself against the measures that follow.

Table 4.2 Assessment: Innovation and entrepreneurship

Behavior	*Self-rating*
Looking at problems from different angles	
Generating novel solutions	
Encouraging others to express a variety of views and ideas	
Encouraging a climate of experimentation and tolerance of mistakes	
Bringing up ideas about future possibilities for the business	
Finding and seizing opportunities to grow the business	
Taking entrepreneurial risks	
Being willing to go against the status quo	

Step 2: Assess Yourself

Using the scale of 1 to 5 (with 1 = Never, 2 = Occasionally, 3 = Often, 4 = Usually, and 5 = Always), rate yourself on how often you follow the eight practices in table 4.2. Think about whether your subordinates would agree with the rating that you are giving yourself. If you foresee a discrepancy between your and your subordinates' ratings, ask yourself why this is so. Then give yourself a final set of ratings that represent a realistic self-appraisal.

Step 3: Take Action

Successive experiences, combined with the desire to be innovative and entrepreneurial, are the best curriculum. In step 1, you made notes for yourself about actions that you were willing to undertake. The best way to practice being innovative and entrepreneurial is to follow through on your own ideas.

One habit that will improve your chances of success is to start a daily journal. This lets you closely track your feelings, thoughts, and actions and the results that you are getting. Regular journal entries bring to the surface connections between your internal private world and your external public world. If your public world is not bringing you the results you want from your initiative, this may call for shifts in your private world of intent, feelings, and thoughts.

In the end, your feelings about your initiative have to be positive. If you do not experience innate satisfaction—as did Shakander, Salman Ali, Ajay, Mr. Kheriya, and Kumarji—you are not likely to stick to your self-improvement plan.

LESSON SEVEN: NAVIGATING POLITICS AND GAINING INFLUENCE

The challenge is to persuade others to see situations in the way that you see them and influence them to think and act in ways that you believe are in the best interests of your organization. As one executive said, "I had a picture of what I wanted to do. But then, merely having the picture is not a solution in itself because you need the support of the entire system to make you successful." Another said, "Evolving as a professional, I realized my mistakes. One is that in the workplace, it's not about having great ideas. It is about pushing through your ideas across many people with such diverse priorities and objectives so as to make something happen." Yet another asked this poignant and pertinent question: "How do you make your organization recognize reality?"

Gaining influence at work follows from waking up to the reality of organizational politics and navigating it. Another way to say this is that politics plays a big part in determining whether leaders will be effective. To gain influence, managers must learn to feel the pulse of politics and use that knowledge to manage their relationships.

Political astuteness involves knowing your organization's norms and policies and how to push the limits when necessary.

Political astuteness also means learning to win support from different parts of the system by conveying conviction and confidence. Importantly, this leadership lesson is about using the power of persuasion to advance one's organization, not one's career. This is one key to overcoming resistance and achieving results. A hallmark of the manager who gains influence against the backdrop of organizational politics is that he or she can talk others into doing things in which they are not that interested initially.

Step 1: Stop and Reflect

We are all born with the capacity to influence others. Even babies and toddlers instinctively bend the actions of other people to meet their own needs and wants. Of course, in our working lives, gaining influence over others is more complicated.

This exercise involves you thinking back across your adult life (including your work and nonwork spheres of influence) to select two memorable incidents—one that showcases you as politically savvy and effective at influencing others; and another that shows you up as lacking political savvy or influencing skills. For example, are there times when you have had your heart set on a goal that you were able *or* unable to achieve? Comparing these two circumstances, think through what factors may have added or detracted from your ability to influence others and bring them around to your point of view. Discuss both situations with a trusted and influential senior colleague or friend to obtain his or her insights, as this will give you perspectives worth treasuring. Your self-assessment follows.

Step 2: Assess Yourself

Using the scale of 1 to 5 (with 1 = Never, 2 = Occasionally, 3 = Often, 4 = Usually, and 5 = Always), rate yourself on the

Table 4.3 Assessment: Navigating politics and gaining influence

Behavior	*Self-rating*
Creating a good impression when meeting people for the first time	
Maintaining relationships with many people within and outside the organization	
Being perceptive about organizational politics	
Persuading others to accept new approaches and ideas	
Influencing others in different situations without using authority or status	

five behaviors in table 4.3. How often do you practice these behaviors?

Step 3: Take Action

How aware are you of the impression you make on others whom you meet professionally? If you do not know, just ask. Include a mix of people, of whom some are flattering and others critical in ways that you may not want to hear. This feedback is likely to motivate you to make changes. If you are already convinced about the benefits of a good first impression, ask yourself this question: what are the one or two things that I most wish to change about how I present myself?

Here are instructive words from a teacher boss who was preparing a junior manager for a head office assignment: "*Wo sub bhul jao*. The first thing is you can't wear dark clothes and half shirts. You have to be well dressed, with a tie and full sleeves, and well groomed, you know. You have to be very presentable, in the way you talk and all that." He then admonished the junior manager to learn to talk softly.

In quoting this teacher boss, I am not suggesting that young managers should thoughtlessly follow someone else's opinion of how to dress, talk, and act. The junior manager in this incident admitted that he did not fully act on the advice given him. What is important is to become aware of one's impact on others at a first meeting, and then make an informed choice about how one wants to present oneself. For example, ask yourself: do you want to show that you are a good listener? Is it important to you to demonstrate your knowledge of your business? Do you want to be seen as conventional or unconventional? Mainly, the impression that you want to create must feel to you like a natural expression of yourself, emanating from who you are.

To begin improving your influencing skills, consider pursuing assignments that involve working across different functions and with people from outside your organization. In these assignments, managers are shorn of their hierarchical power from title, status, formal authority, or expertise. So skills, not power, have to be used to be influential. Examples are:

- serving on a task force to solve a major organizational problem
- managing an annual event that has high visibility
- putting together a coalition of peers to make a recommendation to senior management about introducing a new process or procedures or technology
- working on an entrepreneurial project that requires coordination across the organization
- improving a working relationship with the head of a unit with which your group experiences conflict.[2]

An alternative is to identify an issue or cause about which you feel passionate. Consider, for example, that you want to promote the health benefits of a daily 20-minute walk. Or you want your neighborhood community to become litter free. Or your goal is to educate parents so that they encourage their children to read more and watch less television. Whatever the issue you want to tackle, your passion is a good starting point. As you follow up, you learn about managing political processes and persuading others in your community to take up a course of action from which many can benefit. Your initiative is guaranteed to yield many useful lessons in leadership.

There are other intricate aspects of navigating politics and gaining influence; so this is one lesson that has to be practiced patiently over the years. As managers' influence skills become sophisticated, they can engage more effectively with various stakeholder groups. This leadership lesson is discussed in chapter 5.

IMPLICATIONS FOR INDIAN MANAGERS

The Indian business and economic environment has irrevocably changed from two decades ago. Sweeping reform after liberalization has forced business leaders and managers to innovate and venture into uncharted territories or perish. Veteran managers who have responded successfully to changing times will testify to the rapidity with which they have had to seize opportunities to create something new. For younger managers, fortunate to have a clean slate to create, the present times afford unmatched potential for developing new ideas and exploring the unexplored. New initiatives will only become more pivotal for success as a leader. The lightning speed at which technology is changing is making it necessary to seek new ideas, new methods, and new perspectives relentlessly. Affable relationships with people, agility with ideas, and the willingness to be innovative and entrepreneurial are essential and the best way to learn these is to plunge into the new and unknown. As Rabindranath Tagore said, "You cannot cross the sea merely by standing and staring at the water."[3]

ENDNOTES

1. C. K. Prahalad, *The Fortune at the Bottom of the Pyramid: Eradicating Poverty through Profits* (New Delhi, India: Dorling Kindersley (India) Pvt. Ltd., 2010).
2. C. D. McCauley, *Developmental Assignments: Creating Learning Experiences Without Changing Jobs* (Greensboro, NC: Center for Creative Leadership, 2006).
3. Available at http://www.brainyquote.com/quotes/authors/r/rabindranath_tagore_3.html.

5

THE HORIZONTAL MOVE—JOB ROTATIONS AND TRANSITIONS

> My approach has helped me overall in not becoming bogged down by a new situation, a new workplace, a new industry. Not only can I deliver on targets, I can be energetic and agile. I feel this is this is something that has helped in making me sure of myself wherever I go.
>
> —*Rajkumar Chaddha, president, automotive component manufacturing company*

By talking with senior managers in the 40–60 age range, you will learn that most have worked for one or two organizations for 15–35 or more years. Their career trajectories have been vertical. They rose upward through the ranks by being promoted. The same conversation with managers in their 20s and 30s will display a different career trajectory. In this group, job hopping is more common, with most having worked for several organizations. Others have transitioned from project to project or department to department in one organization. Their assignments were not always a promotion. The younger managers have moved horizontally or sideways, rather than vertically or upward.

A sea change has occurred in how managers view career growth. Those in the 40–60 age bracket tend to be loyalists, preferring to grow within one organization. Those in younger age brackets are far more nimble and willing to move horizontally into different organizations or even different industries.

Without doubt, these moves are professionally exciting because they bring new technical and functional learning and glimpses of alternate leadership styles in other organizational cultures. Horizontal moves, that is, job rotations and transitions, add zest and learning to work life!

There is considerable variety in the horizontal moves that managers make. They can switch (or ask to be switched) from a client-facing role in marketing and sales to an internally oriented operational job; or move from a staff to line function or vice versa. The location of their assignment may change from a metropolis to a town or rural area, simultaneously shifting them from corporate headquarters to field operations, or from administrative roles to shop roles. Some managers go through multiple job transitions between assignments and functions. Finally, in lieu of a horizontal move, managers who participate in project teams that include a cross-section of managers from across their organization learn similar lessons. Their vicarious dip into other functional areas through informal conversations teaches them about the business enterprise. As evident from these examples of horizontal moves, a direct consequence is that managers' *functional and technical expertise* increases.

The distinctive feature of horizontal moves is the managers' exposure to new areas of operation and expertise. They take on responsibilities in an unfamiliar situation, but their level within the hierarchy of their organization (or a different organization) often stays the same. Simply by moving, they see their business through the eyes of different groups of employees and others outside their organization, making it easier for them to look at any situation from multiple perspectives. Such movement confers astuteness at perspective taking: managers learn to handle business situations involving different people with divergent agendas.

There is another potent benefit from horizontal moves. The manager's status and personal power that gradually build in one location in an organization seldom transfer to another location or to another organization. Managers who move have to learn to influence others without their trappings of title. Research at CCL confirms that learning to lead without formal authority is singularly necessary in today's world. Modern global organizations are characterized by flattening hierarchies and permeable boundaries. A new requirement for effectively leading twenty-first-century organizations is to be able to influence others without formal authority. Horizontal moves prepare managers to lead without authority, culminating in their ability to *engage with multiple stakeholders*, as described later in this chapter.

This point cannot be overemphasized: especially for top-level executives, successful leadership is now synonymous with engaging effectively with multiple stakeholders. Competency models allude to this ability in different ways, such as: inclusive leadership, managing diversity, effective cross-cultural communication, multicultural leadership, and ability to collaborate. Based on recent research at CCL, we refer to the ability to work productively with multiple stakeholders as "*boundary-spanning leadership*"—arguably one of the few ways forward for coping with work environments that have become unimaginably interdependent and complex.[1]

We take a behind-the-scenes look at the four circumstances that trigger horizontal moves, noting managers' reactions. Then you are invited to think about whether you wish to add one or several horizontal moves to your portfolio of career experiences.

MEETING BUSINESS NEEDS: WHY ORGANIZATIONS PUSH MANAGERS

Companies usually impose a job rotation on a manager to meet a business need. Superiors push them to overcome their hesitation and take up an assignment in an unfamiliar function. For example, a sales office has to be opened in Shanghai, China, and a manager is temporarily sent across even if he or she does not want such an assignment; or a department head resigns due to family circumstances and a peer is asked to take over his or her job. Unbeknown to them, the managers' potential for taking on a different role has already been recognized by their superiors.

The selected managers react by becoming anxious. They are not confident about their expertise and unsure about whether they can handle the assignment. Their anxiety is compounded by family or colleagues questioning the wisdom of them accepting a horizontal move. The tension between what their organization wants from them and what they expect from themselves is captured by comments from two managers.

Akhilesh said that after three-to-four years in factory production, "I was picked and told that the company felt that 'You will be good in sales as well.' They were not saying that I was not good in the technical functions, but that I would also be good in sales. I laid down my fear that I had not done an MBA—because normally, sales and marketing is the reserved domain for those with MBAs."

Swaroop narrated how "the organization decided that I was a right man to head the business excellence group. I didn't know too much about that. Earlier, I was put in community development; then I was put in HR; and just as I was getting very comfortable with HR and thinking: 'Now I can give back—I've learned a lot and I can give back,' I was moved into uncharted waters. So my fear was that I was not building a core competency in one area, but was just being shifted around. And how much good could that do for me? I was not very sure."

In hindsight, both managers were grateful for being pushed into a career move that they would not have thought about for themselves. Their new roles developed expertise and brought out talents and abilities of which they were unaware. Akhilesh was pleased at adding commercial knowledge to his technical expertise. Building on his cumulative learning from previous experiences, Swaroop learned to create a palpable desire for excellence among his co-workers. This achievement gave him a well-deserved "feeling of euphoria."

Subrata and Gaurav's stories follow; they depict how and what can be learned from moving horizontally. Each of them took on their move for different reasons. Their assignments were dissimilar but their learning was similar. Both came to recognize the value of engaging with stakeholders through many formal and informal communications, and the art of doing so.

Jack of All Trades and the Master of All Trades Too

After graduating with an MBA, Subrata Jolly joined a public sector electronics company. He was young, hardworking, and intelligent. His superiors knew that when he was given a job, Subrata would do it well and on time. So he was handed one opportunity after another—for example, to work with HR and talent recruitment, then to manage office automation, then to develop software, then to carry out consulting assignments, and so forth.

Multiple moves occur frequently in startups and high-growth companies, and Subrata's early career progression was not unusual. He was flexible, learned quickly, and was willing to become multiskilled; so he was transferred rapidly. Subrata acquired a taste for taking on unfamiliar work, and became interested in working in different companies. He switched from his first job in the public sector to a dotcom and then joined a conglomerate. At the conglomerate, his superiors pushed him onto a career path that he knew well. Like the crisscrossing he did on his first job, he once again started to work on projects in different departments, moving among functions and locations.

Then he got assigned to work in a small town, and found himself among a dozen peers who did not hesitate to undermine his credibility and speak ill of him. "When I joined there as senior manager—that was the first time I realized that people can pull you down, and that I had peers whose only objective in life was to ensure that I did not perform well," he said. Up until that time, Subrata had thought of himself as a "loved and protected blue-eyed boy." He believed in being open and fair in his dealing with others. He was used to setting goals and achieving them. This was to be expected, because he had always had resources put in front of him on a silver platter and been given high performance ratings. All his assignments as a young manager had made him shine as an individual, but that phase of his career was behind him. His approach to work did not work any more.

The year that Subrata spent at the conglomerate was very tough, but critical to his growth as a leader. He took nine months to adjust, learning that there were always unstated nuances and motives behind what he was told. He began to understand politics, political processes, and how to work with people with very different agendas. Subrata started to change how he behaved and paid attention to how he was perceived by others. "You have to really manage your environment. I realized that as you go higher, public relations and managing interfaces become critical. In my MBA program, they did not teach me how to manage politics. As they say, this was a different ball game altogether."

The raw learning about managing politics and exercising influence from Subrata's early career years later ripened into a talent for engaging skillfully with stakeholders, specifically due to his many horizontal moves. He subsequently joined a Western multinational company with a subsidiary in India, and then an Indian company that was on its way to becoming global. In both organizations, Subrata's assignments typically lasted for approximately a year. When we caught up with him, he was working in HR, but had already been told that he would be moving to finance.

Over his entire career, Subrata had never asked for a promotion or negotiated on his own behalf. He attributed his successes to two habits. The first was that he was hands on and became completely involved in any task to which he was assigned. This meant that he would devote himself to logical problem solving, gathering inputs from as many people as he could, irrespective of age, status, or seniority. The second was that he was completely willing to learn from subordinates and peers, recognizing that much of the time, their expertise and knowledge were as valuable as his own.

"I mean, anything is possible to achieve," said Subrata. "A lot of influencing needs to be done. I am making it very simple. But I know that what you can achieve wouldn't be possible unless there was mobile technology, because from morning till late night, you make continuous calls from all places. And you have to manage government politicians, friends, customers, suppliers, employees, their families, and all kinds of things. For influencing, the kind of communication we are seeing is enormous. You have to plan and execute multiple things, so it requires strong passion, commitment."

For Subrata, the strategic needs of the different organizations he had joined had meshed nicely with his personal preference for making a contribution and moving on. He saw himself as loyal to his organization but not to a function. The frequency and rapidity of his moves demonstrate that Subrata's bosses recognized that he was proficient at working with and across different groups of stakeholders.

Knowing That You Don't Know

Several senior-level positions had opened up at a conglomerate company, and Gaurav Adhiraj was asked to take up a job as the head of a tough manufacturing business. "And everybody scared me, saying: 'Why are you getting into this? Why could you not ask for another business?' But if you ask me, the key issue was that it was a change for me from the finance stream to the operations stream."

To succeed, Gaurav knew that he needed enough technical expertise to ask the right questions. This stimulated him to become a hands-on leader.

> I used to go to the shopfloor. If they said there was a painting problem [with a particular customer], I would go to the supervisor and ask: "How do you normally paint? How long does it take? What is the problem with this customer? Why is this happening? Why has this not happened in the past?" This is not what people are normally willing to tell you. But there was certain humility in the way I asked. What I am trying to say is that I was not throwing my weight around as the head of the business.

Gaurav then emphasized the importance of becoming approachable, and described his give-and-take style of exchanging information. He would use what he had learned; the suggestions he gave his subordinates came "totally from what I heard from various people and my putting it together in a logical way." But he also used his many one-on-one conversations to listen quietly, cross-examine data and information, become familiar with ground realities, and single-mindedly promote the importance of a profit orientation.

As did Subrata, Gaurav felt that what he learned about working with people would make him effective regardless where he was moved. Gaurav and Subrata's leadership tenets were identical: Be hands on; and be willing to learn. These two tenets merit further discussion. "I didn't go around telling everybody that I don't know anything," said Gaurav. "But I would ask people some questions that would normally seem like you are exposing your ignorance." By his style of exposing some ignorance, Gaurav successfully communicated that he did not know everything but was willing to learn.

For anyone who walks into an unfamiliar situation, one of the best ways to win support is to let stakeholders tell what they know. Both Gaurav and Subrata realized that when managers are willing to learn from stakeholders, their stakeholders are more willing to listen to them. Gaurav and Subrata's experiences tell us that hands-on leadership fused with a learning orientation and commitment to meeting business objectives is extremely effective, especially when managers find themselves in unfamiliar situations.

PREPARING FOR THE FUTURE: USING JOB ROTATIONS TO CULTIVATE AND RETAIN TALENT

Some companies systematically use job rotations to develop their managers. For example, at the Coca-Cola Hellenic Bottling Company in Europe, country general managers are expected to take on two cross-boundary assignments—one outside their function, and the other outside their country of origin.[2] By deliberate rotation, the company exposes its high-potential managers to various aspects of the business and prepares them for senior managerial responsibilities.

A variation is when organizations rotate all their managers through different assignments throughout their careers as a matter of policy. For example, in one Indian financial services company, all managers are rotated through rural assignments. For those born and raised in the major metropolitan areas or cities of India, these assignments are both a horizontal move and an experience of crossing over into a different socio-economic culture, multiplying the leadership lessons learned.

Systematic job rotations are used by organizations to attract and retain top talent too. Newly hired managers are moved through several functions as part of their on-boarding and apprenticeship and a cohort group is created. The cohort then meets from time to time to digest their assignments and deepen their understanding of the company's strategy, culture, and operations. This orientation can take place over several months or for up to a couple of years. A manager who participated in such a program said: "I am grateful to the company for giving me tremendous cross-functional opportunities. I was trained on total quality; I was shifted to finance without any finance experience; and then I went to consulting. I really enjoyed the learning." His remark amplifies how much young managers appreciate this organizational practice.

Managers who are intentionally prepared for leadership responsibilities through job rotations greatly value seeing how the different parts of their organization fit together and the interdependence between functions; this is what gives them a strategic overview of how their organization works and prepares them for senior leadership roles. However, in our study, only a few executives described developmental job rotations, suggesting that this is not a common practice in Indian business organizations.

A MATTER OF CHOICE: THE CASE OF THE CURIOUS MANAGER

According to our study, Indian managers occasionally ask to be transferred to a different function or, what is more likely, move to another organization. Here is a snapshot of managers who orchestrate their own horizontal career moves. They are following their temperamental inclination to investigate how their business works. Stimulated by curiosity, they want to learn about other functions in their business and their industry. Even when superiors or peers are surprised and discourage them from moving, they follow through on an urge to learn and get a holistic view of work life. This is illustrated by the choices Subrata, Dipika, and Ashish made for their careers.

Jack of All Trades and Master of All Trades Too (continued)

Subrata's boss at his first workplace, for example, was not pleased to hear of his interest in moving on to a dotcom. On

Subrata's first day at the dotcom, his executive director and new boss summoned him and urged him to return to his previous job. Apparently, Subrata's previous boss had called his new boss to complain about hiring Subrata away. But this was not the case. Subrata was following his own curiosity and excitement about dotcoms. Despite his sadness at parting from good colleagues and friends, he was not willing to move back. As did Subrata, managers looking to maximize their learning train themselves to manage the emotional side of making a job change.

Following One's Instincts

Dipika Tharoor also liked to follow her curiosity, and took on a cornucopia of projects in her early work life. She eventually joined the financial services industry, and rose rapidly through the ranks.

"After having led several businesses, I chose to opt for operations," said Dipika. "The fact is that driving the business is the glamorous part of any organization. There are sales, ownership, instant limelight, instant recognition, and so forth. To be in the back office is the most unglamorous thing to do. My bosses were actually upset with me for wanting to do back-office work. One of them called me and said, 'What is this nonsense we are hearing? You want to do back-office work?' But it was a turning point, and it gave me a lot of strength."

What is unusual is that Dipika had already been a CEO of several subsidiary businesses. Her bosses were aghast at her decision, telling her: "That is not what we want you to do. You're good at running businesses, and that's what we want you to do." But Dipika took an independent view, believing that it was critical for her to understand the service-oriented operational aspect of her business. She was strengthened by her sense of satisfaction with her own decision. She truly believed that a strong foundation of domain knowledge would help her to reap all the rewards she wanted from the 20-plus years of work life that lay ahead of her.

Always on the Move

Ashish Apte adopted a different tactic for following through on his curiosity. "I started joining many task forces, so I had a sense of what was happening in the other parts of the organization," he confided. "This was not in depth enough for me to say that I could go and do work there on my own immediately. But I got enough of a sense of the issues."

For Subrata, Dipika, and Ashish, new learning—from actual or virtual explorations within and outside their company—was more rewarding than a promotion.

TRANSITIONS: A MIDCAREER HOP FROM ONE INDUSTRY TO ANOTHER

Another choice that some managers make is to change industry. Significant adjustments are made. The learning is enormous, as confirmed by Major Burman and Rajkumar Chaddha.

A Different World

After five years in military school and three years at the National Defence Academy, Major Burman felt totally unprepared for the lack of discipline and gross insubordination among his employees at a public sector bank. "That first couple of years were about trying to readjust to life outside the uniform. To come out from a very regimented, disciplined environment and get into a . . . you know, not so disciplined and not so regimented life called for serious introspection."

Major Burman's previous training had come from senior officers who were winners of the Param Vir Chakra and Mahavir Chakra awards. His coursework, which was personally fascinating for him, covered thousands of years of war history and its implications for leadership. He tried to incorporate some of the principles he had learned into his leadership style, which made him a misfit at the bank. No one could understand why he was so courteous to customers!

"You know, something that people would often ask me was: 'Why are you being so good to that fellow?' I would say: 'I am not being good to him, I am being normal.' I just thought that they were other human beings and that when you interact with others, you have to be polite and civil."

The crossover from a military to nonmilitary work life gave him a mind-opening perspective on people, increasing his commitment to provide outstanding customer service. Later in his career, Major Burman was able to act on his commitment more completely. He used his disciplined and disciplinary approach to instill a service-oriented work ethic at the government bank branch that he managed, despite the trade union-induced disorder that prevailed at that time.

Learning Agility Pays Off for Rajkumar Chaddha

Rajkumar Chaddha's career was dotted with transitions too. To an even greater extent than Subrata, he had made multiple cross-industry crossovers by choice. What he learnt about succeeding in a new work environment validates Subrata and Gaurav's leadership tenets—a hands-on, learning-oriented style that focuses on business objectives is tremendously motivating for employees and stakeholders.

But Rajkumar went an extra step and advanced their seminal insights into the art of facilitative leadership. He described how his style was *not* "command and demand," because he was most often in situations where his subordinates were almost his father's age or older.

"Although I have changed only three industries, this is now the eighth factory where I am working," observed Rajkumar.

> I like the way these opportunities come more often to me. I keep it simple. I keep people involved, and work as a facilitator. If people are open, transparent, and upfront, and say what has to be said, that is better. I also make sure our team is motivated and happy—working and delivering. I think if one gets into a new industry or is dealing with very experienced direct reports, one has to work as a facilitator. I mean, we are not the technological expert. So, we have to facilitate positive thinking, facilitate teamwork, facilitate creativity . . . you take people along by giving space for people to work, as well as keeping control. We give confidence, and we give both challenge and support. See, if I am new in an industry, I can always demand that which has never happened before because I don't know what is possible and not possible.

As expressed by the opening quotation for this chapter, Rajkumar is buoyantly self-assured about his ability to facilitate necessary actions to meet business goals. He knows his approach guarantees him huge success in dealing with situations in which he has limited expertise.

LESSON EIGHT: ENGAGING WITH MULTIPLE STAKEHOLDERS

In management literature, the word "stakeholder" broadly includes all persons and groups affected by a decision or activity. Business organizations have an array of stakeholders—managers, their bosses and peers, employees, suppliers and distributors, the general public, and of course, the families of these people.

Managing multiple stakeholders is not easy. Leaders must merge conflicting hopes and priorities, contain tensions and insecurities, meet business objectives, and advance their organization and industry. Perceptions and expectations have to be reconciled. Policies and decisions must be made acceptable and implemented. Public communications have to be timely and accurate, so that the manager can lobby effectively to win people over to his or her point of view. The emotional and anxious reactions of individuals or groups have to be handled with maturity, with individual egos assuaged.

Horizontal moves open the door to learning the basics of engaging with stakeholders. How does this happen? When directing others' work and activities, managers face two possibilities: either their status within their organization gives them the authority to direct others; or they must direct others without having authority over them. While the leadership task in both cases involves directing others, there are critical differences in the leadership style that will be most effective.

With stakeholders, managers usually cannot use title and status-based authority. In Rajkumar's words, they cannot "command and demand" because they will not be effective if they do so. Horizontal moves land managers in similar circumstances, inasmuch as they cannot count on formal authority to direct others. So they have to behave in ways that win over co-workers.

The behaviors that are effective will be described shortly, after an invitation to you to consider your level of interest in a horizontal move.

Step 1: Pause and Reflect

Imagine that you are preparing for an interview on a business-oriented TV talk show. The talk show host is focusing on the impact of job rotations and job hopping on your career. She has provided you with a list of questions that she will ask in her 30-minute conversation with you. Here is that list.

- How often have you rotated from job to job in your company or job hopped from one company to another?
- What motivated you to do so?
- Which one of your job rotations or job-hopping experiences stands out as the most memorable? What made it memorable?

- What did you gain from that experience, personally and professionally?
- Do you see any disadvantage to rotating from job to job or job hopping?
- What have you learned about yourself from moving around?
- What did you learn about leadership that you can share with others who are planning a similar move?
- Any final thoughts before we welcome our next guest?

Preparing for this interview lets you draw on your own experiences. If horizontal moves have not been a part of your career, you can approach one or two colleagues or friends who have moved or been moved. Become the interviewer and ask them the questions on the talk show host's list. What you learn from interviewing colleagues or friends will add depth and detail to what you have read in this chapter. Armed with this knowledge, you can determine your level of readiness for engaging with multiple stakeholders inside and outside your place of work.

Step 2: Assess Yourself

Using the scale of 1 to 5 (with 1 = Never, 2 = Occasionally, 3 = Often, 4 = Usually, and 5 = Always), rate yourself on the seven behaviors in table 5.1. How often do you practice these behaviors? Would your stakeholders agree with the rating that you are giving yourself? Keeping this in mind, come up with your final ratings.

Step 3: Take Action

If you are interested in developing your ability to engage with stakeholders, which behaviors do you wish to cultivate first? Perhaps you need to meet with stakeholders more frequently. If

Table 5.1 Assessment: Engaging with multiple stakeholders

Behavior	*Self-rating*
Communicating regularly with stakeholders	
Handling skeptical or negative stakeholder attitudes firmly and diplomatically	
Carefully listening to multiple perspectives before addressing an issue	
Managing strong emotions between groups effectively Using appropriate transparency when communicating with stakeholders	
Communicating effectively by accurately sensing when to listen and when to talk	
Gaining commitment from different groups by sharing an inspiring vision	

you already spend enough time communicating with them, ask yourself whether you handle the negative attitudes of some stakeholders with composure. As a manager, do you listen to others' opinions and ideas first or do you prefer to start by presenting your opinions and ideas? Which seems to be more effective? How driven are you to be influential by devoting the necessary time and energy to achieve this?

In today's world, leaders have to influence people over whom they have little or no authority. No matter how small the steps you take, your best option is to start down the path that improves your ability to engage with stakeholders. I predict that your small successes will give you a rush of feelings of satisfaction. In turn, these feelings will motivate you to double your efforts to engage effectively with multiple stakeholders.

IMPLICATIONS FOR INDIAN MANAGERS

Horizontal moves impart a wealth of expertise on a wide spectrum of functions, while also making managers adept at dealing with different kinds of people. The logic that supports gaining the multiple perspectives made possible by such moves can be traced to Chanakya's *Arthashastra*, written more than 2,300 years ago.

The *Arthashastra*, a world-renowned, primary treatise on statecraft, economic policy, and military strategy, sets forth the ideal of *rajarshi*. Composed from two Sanskrit words, *raja*, or king, and *rishi*, or sage, the *rajarshi* is a wise and virtuous king. The philosopher–king model proposed by Socrates and Plato expresses a similar message—that the secular world is ideally managed through the evolved vision of a philosopher or sage.[3]

One of the essential qualities of a *rajarshi* is that of "improving his own discipline by (continuing his) learning in all branches of knowledge." Furthermore, "he should be well trained in all the arts and be able to lead the army." Of the king's ability to manage internal strife, Chanakya says, "Quarrels among people can be resolved by winning over the leaders or by removing the cause of the quarrel."[4]

This ancient wisdom regarding the need for the king to acquire learning in all branches of knowledge and become well versed in the arts and in military strategy parallels what is necessary for effective leadership of business organizations today. Chanakya's counsel about abilities that kings must attain corresponds to skills that develop from horizontal moves: a well-rounded perspective on how the different parts of the organizational kingdom function; and skillfulness at thinking both holistically and strategically. The *rajarshi*'s ability to resolve differences by winning over leaders or removing the cause of the quarrel is akin to the business leader engaging successfully with diverse stakeholders, albeit, in comparison with contemporary business leaders, the *rajarshi* seems to operate from a position of greater moral authority. Horizontal moves, apparently, could be one pathway to becoming a modern-day *rajarshi*, or, I propose, a *ranirshi*.

ENDNOTES

1. C. Ernst, C. & D. Chrobot-Mason, *Boundary Spanning Leadership: Six Practices for Solving Problems, Driving Innovation, and Transforming Organizations* (New York: McGraw-Hill Professional, 2010). Boundary-spanning leadership is the capability to create direction, alignment, and commitment across boundaries in service of a higher vision or goal. CCL research conducted in India and across six world regions—Africa, Asia, Europe, the Middle East, North America, and South America—has identified six boundary-spanning practices that encourage collaboration across a range of boundaries.
2. APQC, *Leadership Development Strategy: Linking Strategy, Collaborative Learning, and Individual Leaders* (Houston: APQC, 2006).
3. S.K. Chakaraborty, *Ethics in Management: Vedantic Perspectives* (New Delhi: Oxford University Press, 1995).
4. Kautilya, *Arthashastra*. Available at http://wapedia.mobi/en/Arthashastra.

6

CROSSING CULTURES

> I do not want my house to be walled in on all sides and my windows to be stuffed. I want the cultures of all the lands to be blown about my house as freely as possible. But I refuse to be blown off my feet by any.
>
> —*Mohandas Karamchand Gandhi*[1]

> It was important for me to modify my lifestyle and my style. I found that to be effective, I had to be flexible. And simply to say: "This is the way I am, take it or leave it"—that's almost like committing *hara kiri* in an international culture.
>
> —CEO, *tractor manufacturing company*

In just the way that M. K. Gandhi and other broad-minded political leaders have embraced all world cultures, business leaders are doing so too. These well-known comments from Gandhi, juxtaposed with those from Vinod (a culturally savvy CEO of a tractor manufacturing company), bring up a question that conscientious global leaders have to ask themselves: is it possible to bend and sway with the winds of other cultural mores without losing balance and being blown off one's feet?

We will return to Vinod's story later in this chapter. Here, his remarks introduce the dilemma that is thrust upon managers who want to lead effectively in other cultures. Words and actions that are second nature to them have to be reconsidered and sometimes changed, posing emotional and deeply personal challenges. Valued beliefs are tested to the nth degree and have to be selectively adjusted. Adjustments are the essence of cultural adaptability, without which it is impossible to lead and work with people from other cultures.

Lest this statement seem too fervent, consider these contradictions and their implications. In formal cultures, when managers are asked to introduce themselves, they give their full name, title, and a fairly detailed account of their responsibilities; in informal cultures, managers use their first name, and joke about their title and responsibilities. Imagine the first teleconference between IT professionals hailing from formal and informal cultures. After the meeting, can their team leader counter the formal team's dismay about their informal colleagues' immaturity, or curb the informal team's laughter at the almost pompous seriousness of their formal colleagues?

Another example of cultural differences is in how decisions get made. A manager working in Asia started his career at a Japanese automotive company. He described an awkward moment that occurred a few years later, when he accepted a senior position in an organization in the U.K., his home country. Following practices he had learned in Japan, he called his management team together to arrive at a consensual decision, and was taken aback by his team's strongly negative reactions. They believed that the decision was his to make, that he was wasting their time, and that he was expecting them to do the job for which he was getting paid.

Consider also differences concerning who is expected to contribute opinions at a meeting, and who is not. Hierarchical cultures often use one spokesperson, and are disturbed by meetings in nonhierarchical cultures, in which individuals feel free to express their views, and frequently do.

Then there is the case of behaviors that are admired in one culture, but not in another. Conditioned by cultural upbringing, leaders from some countries see themselves as efficient, tactical, and business oriented. To their chagrin, they later realize that co-workers from other cultures have interpreted their behavior as showing that they lack fellow feeling, and are hasty and rude.

There are countless such examples of cultural mores that are at odds. Moving to another country, or even to another part of India, can involve not only foreseeable adjustments to climate, geography, food, clothing, secular and religious holiday celebrations, language, and social and business customs; there are also unforeseeable adaptations that are outside our awareness. Unsurprisingly, some amount of misunderstanding and friction between managers from different cultures is inevitable. So what can managers do to be better prepared to untangle cultural miscommunications and lead in a global context?

Training programs, short courses, and books that aim to improve cultural knowledge and interactions are widely available. But the main point of this chapter is not that managers need to become cultural specialists, but that cultural adjustments have to be made to achieve business goals. Bridging cultural differences is not about mastering a vast and intricate topic, but about a state of mind. This state of mind is demonstrated outwardly by managers' interest in getting to know the views and practices of co-workers who are different from them.

THE RELEVANCE OF CULTURAL ADAPTABILITY AND CROSS-CULTURAL SAVVY TO LEADERSHIP EFFECTIVENESS

Culture is a unique worldview shared among a group of people. Managers' worldviews—often referred to as the software of the mind—are a patchwork of beliefs that have been absorbed from their family, school and college, social and professional networks, and the community and country to which they belong. Worldviews generate a collective way of thinking, feeling, and acting. They serve an important purpose—worldviews help a group to bond and belong with each other and to adapt together to their changing environment.[2]

Culturally adaptable managers are able to move back and forth between groups with different worldviews more easily. This implies that they can reflect on their habits of thinking and acting and experiment with alternatives. This is similar to people donning different apparel. For example, by changing into sports gear, a business suit, evening gala wear, a cook's apron, or a *kurta-pajama*, a person becomes mentally prepared for physical exercise, for work, for a social evening, for cooking a special meal, or for relaxation. Each is a separate sphere of activity, and the clothes are a way of entering into diverse worlds of action and feeling. For most of us, moving between two or more cultural environments is not as easy as changing clothes. But for those who are open to making adjustments, crossing cultures can ultimately become as easy as changing clothes.

Cross-cultural savvy grows out of cultural adaptability. Cross-cultural savvy is the ability to work effectively in other cultures due to sufficient knowledge about people, business practices, and social customs. Adaptable managers are able to learn what they need to know more quickly. For example, adaptable Indian managers working in the U.S. rapidly learn to be assertive and communicate openly and directly. Comfortable with trying on different worldviews and behaviors, adaptable managers become catalysts of their own continual cross-cultural learning, which readies them for senior roles in global organizations.

There is a mammoth payoff to their organizations. Senior executives claim that cross-cultural savvy among the management team conspicuously improves business operations and growth.

Here is a simple framework that displays the layers of proficiency built up by effective business leaders through years of assignments.

Effective leadership = Technical/functional/
professional expertise
+ Managerial expertise
+ Business expertise
+ Cross-cultural expertise/savvy[3]

The framework clarifies that cross-cultural savvy is only one component of effectiveness. But senior Indian leaders with international and cross-regional work experience confirm that the cross-cultural component is hugely consequential to the global business success of their companies.

We note that cross-cultural assignments immerse managers in torrential possibilities for new learning: cutting-edge technical learning; managerial learning, such as navigating a new initiative or job rotation; business learning, such as knowledge about the legalities of company or office formation and incorporation, import and export regulations, or licensing agreements; and cultural savvy, since they will have to work with superiors, peers, and subordinates who talk and act differently from them. In this chapter, we focus on cross-cultural adaptation and learning (rather than business, managerial, or technical learning).

For leaders preparing to cross cultures, five vignettes follow. These are an indicative, not exhaustive, set of examples illustrating potentially problematic situations. The vignettes are snapshots of circumstances in which cross-cultural savvy had to be learned. They portray how so-called "normal" behaviors by Indian managers triggered unexpected and potentially conflict-creating reactions. Fortunately, these managers' faux pas were caught in time and yielded cultural savvy, helping them to manage more effectively.

The vignettes are linked to rituals that smoothen out cross-cultural interactions. Rituals regularize social conduct.[4] For example, in India, rituals include always greeting others with *namaste* or offering visitors *chai*. These and other prescriptions for social behavior harmonize relationships. The rituals in this chapter are tried-and-true ways of absorbing another culture's perspectives and practices. These rituals tone up *cultural adaptability* and build bridges of understanding between managers and workers from different cultures.

The message from the vignettes and rituals is that miscommunication and misunderstandings are to be expected, but can be managed and turned around. You are invited to consider your motivation and interest in inculcating a spirit of adaptability, which is the basis of respectful and trusting relationships with co-workers from other countries. These relationships are the source of cross-cultural savvy, which comes from willingness to learn with and from others who are different.

FROM THE UNKNOWN TO THE KNOWN: CRAFTING CULTURAL SAVVY

The vignettes illustrate how crossing cultures is not easy. Generally, people do not know what they do not know about a different culture. We make mistakes without knowing that we are making mistakes.

Right or Wrong: a Misunderstanding on the Technology Transfer Project

Sumeeta's Indian and U.K. subordinates were working on a technology transfer project. The U.K. production manager made a proposal; his Indian counterpart told him that his approach was wrong. The U.K. production manager was taken aback at being told so directly that he was wrong, and stopped talking. He was very offended. Sumeeta had to talk with each of them, and then set up a meeting for both of them to talk with each other. "How do we try to understand each other and learn to modify our behaviors?" she asked.

As a result of their difficult conversation, the U.K. production manager came to understand that his Indian colleague was expressing himself in the same way as he would with colleagues back home. The Indian learned that there are other ways of expressing disagreement that would be more acceptable to a manager who had grown up in the U.K. After their conversation, the men became good friends, working effectively for two months on the project, and joining each other in after-work activities.

Ritual #1: Pay attention to emotions. Cross-cultural encounters can induce strong emotional reactions because the behavior of others can easily be misinterpreted and judged negatively. When negative emotions are not tactfully brought to the surface, they stay hidden behind a polite face, but create chains of negative thoughts and actions. Managers on a cultural crossing have to be on the watch for emotional reactions, which may need to be neutralized with good humor and mutual apologies, while preserving the dignity of those involved.

Ritual #2: Proactively resolve misunderstandings and conflicts. Some misunderstanding or conflict is part of all human interactions, but especially cross-cultural ones. There are innocent oversights, confusion over language, misinterpretations of intent, deep-seated animosities between people from different backgrounds that erupt in seemingly neutral interactions, and myriad unexpected triggers for negative or even hostile feelings. Therefore, the ability to manage, work through, and contain or resolve misunderstandings and conflicts is paramount for business productivity. The Indian and U.K. subordinates were fortunate that their culturally savvy boss Sumeeta intervened just in time.

Ritual #3: Ask for feedback, and provide feedback if asked. By talking with each of them individually, and encouraging them to talk with each other, Sumeeta made it possible for the two managers to give each other feedback. Feedback can be as simple as each person taking turns to share the impact of the other's behavior on him or her sincerely. Honest sharing creates strong bonds of trust. "Feedback," in such instances, tells managers how they are perceived by someone from another country or culture, and gives them the chance to change their behavior.

Interruptions

When working in the U.S. and the U.K., Ravi found that he had to ask for an appointment even if he wanted to have a five-minute exchange of ideas. In India, even when he was in the middle of something, he was comfortable with being interrupted for several minutes, resolving an issue, and then getting on with the work at hand. But he learned that for some of the non-Indians with whom he worked, a brief interruption was a major disturbance.

Ritual # 4: Synchronize communication protocols. Intercultural work involves multiple languages and multiple ways of using language. Styles of communication vary. For example, Indians are wont to interrupt each other in conversations. In several cultures, this is considered rude. In yet other cultures, the norm is to pause before making one's own comments, to show that the other person's remarks have been carefully considered.

To connect with other people, managers must begin to sense when to pause, when to interrupt, and how to use humor, if at all. Sagacious judgments must be made about which language to use when colleagues are mono, bi-, or multilingual to avoid giving offence. Even managers who speak the same language, such as English, may use idioms and expressions that are incomprehensible to the other. To be in sync with people from another culture, astute global managers learn to be mindful of what is said and what is *not* said. They also learn to listen to tone, and observe nonverbal gestures and general body language. The vignette involving Vinod (which follows) illustrates why managers on cross-cultural assignments must be mindful about communication protocols, and how that can affect their leadership.

Ritual #5: Find and use cultural brokers. Ravi was intrigued by how managers react differently to interruptions. This, and the other communication style differences that he observed, prompted him to enroll in a three-day program on culturally competent communications. Ravi's work experience, observations, coursework, and thoughtfulness set him up to be a cultural broker. For Indians on expatriate assignments to other countries, or managers from other countries coming to India, he can be a tutor on how to avoid communication mishaps. He can also facilitate connections to key people in the countries in which he has worked, and is interested in doing so. A general caveat is that cultural brokers have valuable insights, but their opinions may not represent the viewpoints of other cultural insiders.

"Yes" or "No": I Don't Know

Vinod's preferred managerial style was to be transparent and direct with his opinions. Growing up in India, his tendency was to say out loud whatever was on his mind. He expected others to have the same style, but realized that was a dictatorial expectation. He was working in Indonesia at the time. The Javanese in Indonesia are harmony oriented and consensual. "Normal" discussions and acceptable arguments in India would be construed as confrontations by them. So his subordinates were just not going to tell him what was on their mind.

Vinod learned to read people—to infer what his subordinates were trying to tell him from their tone of expression and body signals. He began to sense resistance or boredom; and by close observation, he could tell whether a subordinate was disagreeing or merely disinterested in what he was saying.

Upon reflection, he realized that his management style was both Western and Asian. On the one hand, he used logic and believed in examining issues dispassionately and in a direct and open way. On the other hand, he was aware that at heart, he was Asian, not always "clinically professional," and more likely to take matters personally. As did his Indonesian counterparts, he felt he had inhibitions about sharing personal feelings. His reflections changed his behavior. "My managerial style has softened as a result, and I have become a better manager," said Vinod.

Ritual #6: Restrain dictatorial expectations. One of the main obstacles to productive boss–subordinate relationships (when bosses and subordinates are from different cultures) is that bosses often react emotionally, based on a fixed mental model of "how things should be." This is why Vinod expected his subordinates to tell him what was on their minds. This expectation was so deeply embedded in him as to be invisible to him initially. To his credit, he restrained himself from dictatorial insistence that his subordinates behave as he wanted! This gave him the chance to think and adjust.

Ritual #7: Practice reflection to gain self-insight. Vinod was also savvy enough to take the time to reflect. Intercultural interactions place the manager in situations that are unfamiliar and frequently uncomfortable. If the manager is open, this disequilibrium provides a chance for new knowledge, especially about oneself. Reflection clarifies personal preferences and values. Vinod was ready to learn. His willingness to question his own assumptions and make adjustments is part of what made him an effective leader.

Who Is the Boss?

Sujeet observed that his Indian general manager "did not feel very good" when his American subordinates addressed him by his first name. This reminded Sujeet of when he had worked in Mexico. There, he was the boss, but the operators would all sit with their legs on the table, and call Sujeet by his first name.

"I felt hurt that they were not respecting me," he said. But he came to realize that "they did still consider me their boss and listened to me."

Ritual #8: Show tolerance by withholding hasty judgments. At the heart of tolerance is willingness to suspend judgment about others' behaviors and values. Sujeet tolerated his Mexican subordinates using his first name and putting their feet up in front of him. By mulling over the situation, he created cultural savvy for himself. As did Vinod, he accepted different behaviors, and thought about his own preferences and values before choosing a course of action. He benefited by not being hasty.

Sujeet made it possible for his subordinates to candidly exchange information with him. When employees with so-called lower status and less power are shown respect, there are rewards: knowledge sharing and learning become multidirectional. Multidirectional learning is a turbo engine that drives cross-cultural insights and leader effectiveness. A general attitude of respect for other cultures, people, and practices is crucial for successful relationships.

My Way or Your Way

Sridhar, an Indian manager working outside India in the Southeast Asian region, wanted to promote a product by using an ad campaign that had been very successful in several other countries. The ad had portrayed a typical mother-in-law and daughter-in-law scenario, and he was sure that the theme would work. He did not want his regional ad campaign team to reinvent the marketing wheel, and strongly urged them to adapt the ad.

From their polite objections and go-slow tactics, he sensed real reluctance. To him, the team's resistance seemed to come from their desire to create something new, and their feelings that they were the experts on their own region. Although the ad had worked in Japan, the U.S., India, the Scandinavian countries, and the U.K., the team did not want to assume that it would work in their sales territory too.

Sridhar told himself that he had to respect the ad campaign team's individuality and creativity. If he ceded to their ideas, he would gain more in terms of building long-term trust. So even though he had the authority to push the original ad through, he backpedalled and let them go in the direction they wanted. He knew he had not handled the situation perfectly, but he learned from that incident and promised himself he would handle similar situations differently in the future. What mattered is that his non-Indian, multicultural team and Sridhar had a common goal, and Sridhar gave them the freedom to meet that common goal in their own way.

Ritual #9: Create commitment using common goals. Common goals and shared commitments are a solid foundation for relationships. Managers and employees who passionately want to achieve the same goals usually find ways to communicate, build mutual respect and trust, and work through conflicts, because they believe that doing so will help them achieve what they all want. Sridhar and his team had a common goal—creating a successful ad campaign.

The next time you find yourself in a fractious cross-cultural situation, one or more of these rituals may make your cultural crossing less bumpy. Caution is necessary, however. Cultures are dynamic and evolve continually. Managers are a mix of thoughts and feelings produced not just by culture and community, but also by the idiosyncrasies of their upbringing and personality. When different ways of talking and acting are encountered, it would be a mistake to assume too quickly that the source of that difference is "culture."

We move on to see how cross-cultural savvy is learned; and you are invited to develop your own way of resolving cross-cultural dilemmas by using the rituals and the information that follows.

LESSON NINE: CROSS-CULTURAL SAVVY

Cross-cultural learning is deeply personal. Fundamental values and preferences are called into question. Conceptually, it is easy to grasp that business and cultural norms outside India are different. Emotionally, experiencing the differences raises a flood of intense, conflicting feelings. Behaviorally, a great deal of reflection and effort are needed for sorting out which adjustments to make, and when and how to make them.

In today's global economy, exposure to different cultures is easily possible, with bountiful opportunities to practice adaptability and become culturally savvy. Without leaving India, managers can work for an Indian company, but in a different region from the one they grew up and were schooled in. Or they can accept a position with a foreign multinational—for example, a branch or subsidiary of a French, Norwegian, or Japanese parent company. They can be regional general managers or functional heads residing in India, with responsibilities for regional or international operations. Of course, managers can also relocate to a foreign country.

The potential for cross-cultural learning is independent of the managers' realm of job responsibilities. They can pursue cultural learning from their position as an intern, a technical expert, consultant, company representative, or participant in an educational or training opportunity. The most advantageous situation is when managers are exposed to cultural diversity early in life, and watch people with status and authority (such as elder family members, bosses, superiors and community leaders) accept and appreciate people from different backgrounds. But mid and late career managers can become culturally savvy too.

The following "stop and reflect" exercises are potent when a small group of managers—with some experience of living and working in a different culture—form a self-learning group.

Step 1: Stop and Reflect

The first stage starts with all the people in the group taking a few quiet minutes by themselves to recall and list several cross-cultural incidents in their own lives. These are situations in which they became intensely conscious that there are people who think, feel, and act differently from them. The incident could have happened during primary school, for example when they were told not to play with children from another ethnic or socioeconomic group. Perhaps an incident occurred during a holiday visit to relatives with different food habits. Since diversity is ubiquitous in India, many stories from high school, college, or one's career will be remembered.

In the second stage, everyone pairs up to exchange stories. From their list, each person selects *one* incident that aroused considerable emotion in him or her, such as surprise, frustration, embarrassment, anger, or delight. The partners take turns telling their story. The storyteller describes what happened. Who were the people involved? What did each person say or do? How did others react? What was the outcome? Most importantly, the storyteller talks about his or her feelings and opinions about what happened earlier in his or her life. Last, he or she notes whether there was any learning from the incident. Meanwhile, the listener interrupts only to ask clarifying questions.

In the third stage (after the stories have been told), all the pairs join and form a group. A few members volunteer to tell their own story, or to let their partner tell his or her story. Here is what is essential. After each story is told, group members speculate about what drove the words and actions of all the people in each story; meanwhile, the person who "owns" the story remains silent and listens. For example, if Sujeet (from the vignette about "Who Is the Boss?") is narrating his experience, these questions could be raised and answered in the group while Sujeet stayed silent: what were the drivers for the behavior of his Mexican subordinates? Were the subordinates testing

Sujeet? Are there other ways in which Sujeet could have handled his Mexican subordinates? Regarding the reactions of his Indian boss, is he being overly sensitive?

The critical skill to learn is that of generating many possible explanations or interpretations of what occurred. When the exchange of opinions has reached a natural stopping point, the "owner" of the story is invited to share his or her views.

In the fourth and final stage, the discussion becomes scenario oriented. The group collectively mulls over the alternate ways in which the people in the story could have behaved. They create scenarios of how different behaviors would have led to different outcomes. For example, if Sujeet had confronted his Mexican subordinates, how might they have reacted? What are some of the scenarios and consequences from what Sujeet does with his perceptions about his general manager? For example, what actions could Sujeet take or not take to respond to his Indian boss' predicament? One or several roleplays are scripted and acted out to show how the story could have a different and satisfying ending.

Storytelling and retelling are not trivial activities. Cultivating the habit of viewing an emotionally charged situation from different angles in and of itself is a way to disentangle misunderstandings mentally. By pausing, rewinding, and replaying the scene over several times, new questions come up about the incident, and wiser possibilities for future action emerge. Insights can be used to push "reset," change oneself, and recalibrate the current situation, as Sujeet did in his handling of his Mexican subordinates. Or the manager can behave differently in a future situation, which is what Sridhar told himself to do in the vignette on "My Way or Your Way."

The point to consider is whether we want to learn from others and adapt our own thoughts and actions—without losing our anchor in our own identity of course. Next you can assess your willingness to learn and adapt, because this is the pathway to cultural savvy.

Table 6.1 Assessment: Cross-cultural savvy

Behavior	*Self-rating*
Seeking out opportunities to work with people from different backgrounds	
Learning business and social etiquette quickly when assigned to a new culture	
Adjusting some of my behaviors to fit into a new culture	
Being curious about different worldviews and values	
Taking enjoyment from experiencing different cultures	

Step 2: Assess Yourself

Using the scale of 1 to 5 (with 1 = Never, 2 = Occasionally, 3 = Often, 4 = Usually, and 5 = Always), rate yourself on the five behaviors in table 6.1. How often do you practice these behaviors?

Step 3: Take Action

Based on what you have learned about yourself, you can form an action plan. The telling and retelling of stories must be included as part of your plan, since stories are a primary means of learning about other cultures. Some Korean companies have established databases with stories about their managers' experiences outside Korea, and what was learned. The database then helps others to prepare themselves when assigned outside Korea.

Another means of cross-cultural learning is to pay attention to others' blunders, so you can reduce your own slips, slides, and falls on a cultural crossing. CCL is currently developing *Global Leader View* (GLV), an assessment instrument that helps leaders see the gaps between what co-workers from other cultures are looking for in a leader and what they themselves deliver. For cross-cultural managers, it is worth noting where mismatches between culture-based expectations and the leader's demonstrated style will cause co-workers to assess the leader as not up to the mark. Based on GLOBE[5], an extensive international research project, the six dimensions along which there is culture-based variation in leadership style are:

- *Authority oriented:* leader influences others by formal status, authority or position.
- *Autonomous:* leader is independent, individualistic, or self-reliant.
- *Charismatic:* leader inspires others around a vision or values and high performance standards.
- *Humane oriented:* leader is supportive, compassionate, and considerate of others.
- *Participative:* leader shares power and decision making.
- *Team oriented:* leader effectively builds and manages cohesive and loyal teams that work to achieve a common goal.

The GLOBE confirms that good leadership is in the eye of the beholder, and culture is one of the lenses used. This is why it is important to learn from cultural brokers and from others with whom you can talk in depth. Conversations can help you to anticipate what you need to do to adjust, so that your business goals can be achieved.

Besides conversing with others, here is a list of preparatory assignments that will stimulate your personal development: working with a diverse project team in one's own country; relocation to a different region in one's country; trips abroad for business or pleasure; leading or participating on a virtual and multicountry project team; working for a skillful international manager; or expatriation.[6]

The central purpose of all the storytelling, assessment, conversations, and assignments is well articulated by this wise and cross-culturally savvy leader:

> With my job in international marketing, when I have to meet someone from another country (in the Far East, the Middle East, or Africa), I make it a point to learn about their culture and their traditions. I like to read and make sure that I avoid doing something wrong that will be offensive. I have found that human beings all over the world are the same—they respond to warmth, genuineness, honesty, and integrity. They respond when they realize that while promoting your organization, you are also trying to help their organization. I think that is the key to building trust with your clients, after which business is automatic.

At the end of the day, cross-cultural savvy is intertwined with mutual respect and trust. Trust is of the essence in intercultural relationships. This is especially true in light of the ever-present likelihood of conflict and misunderstanding. In conflict situations, trust may be the one thing that gives people the psychological space to work through their problems. However, trust, particularly at the beginning of a relationship, cannot be assumed and has to be earned. While trust is difficult to earn, it is also fragile and can be easily sundered by experiences that may seem insignificant to some and very significant to others.

IMPLICATIONS FOR INDIAN MANAGERS

The past decade has seen unprecedented consolidation and expansion by Indian businesses, including successful acquisitions of foreign-owned companies. So while there is jubilation at the Tata Group's takeover of Tetley or Corus, and cheers when Rediff.com is listed on foreign bourses, these moves imply that future leaders of Indian businesses will have to cultivate cross-cultural savvy. The challenges are not only to adapt personally to different cultures, but to lead diverse teams from a workforce with varied cultural backgrounds.

In a country with 18 official languages and 28 states (at last count), most urban Indians grow up amid people speaking dozens of languages, and following a variety of lifestyles, forms of worship, culinary preferences, and fashions. This unique sociocultural environment gives Indians a natural advantage at accommodating diversity and adapting to different cultures. But being adaptable and becoming culturally savvy are always a matter of personal choice; and the story that follows brings the nature of this choice to the foreground.

> Long ago, there was a Chakravarti; his kingdom stretched to the horizon. He was the ruler of 12 nations. And people of these different nations spoke different languages. The Chakravarti was growing old, so one day he called his two sons. He said, "I am the ruler of 12 nations and my people speak in 12 languages and many more dialects. Therefore, they often fight with each other and do not understand each other. How should we remedy this?" One son said, "Let us impose upon them a single language, so that all of them speak the same language and understand each other. That will surely bring peace." The other son said, "I disagree, I will not impose a single language upon them. I shall instead learn all 12 languages, so that I can understand all the 12 peoples and settle the disputes between them and that way all 12 will look upon me as the great king. That way, each nation will retain its own identity and will be very different from the other." The king smiled and said to the second son, "You shall be my heir because your kingdom shall last longer."[7]

ENDNOTES

1. M. K. Gandhi, *The Collected Works of Mahatma Gandhi*, VI, 1-6-1921, p. 170. Available at http://archaeology.about.com/od/quotations/qt/quote164.htm.

2. M. S. Wilson, Effective Cross-Cultural Leadership: Tips and Techniques for Developing Capacity. In: N. A. Boyacigiller, R. A. Goodman, & M. E. Phillips, (eds.), *Crossing Cultures: Insights from Master Teachers* (New York and London: Routledge, 2003).
3. M. S. Wilson & M. A. Dalton, *International Success: Selecting, Developing and Supporting Expatriate Managers* (Greensboro, NC: Center for Creative Leadership, 1998). Adapted with permission.
4. J. Stein (editor in chief), *The Random House Dictionary of the English Language: The Unabridged Edition* (New York, NY: Random House, 1967).
5. P. Dorfman, P. J. Hanges, & F. C. Brodbeck, Leadership and Cultural Variation: The Identification of Culturally Endorsed Leadership Profiles. In R. J. House, P. J. Hanges, M. Javidan, P. Dorfman, & V. Gupta (eds.), *Leadership, Culture, and Organisations: The GLOBE Study of 62 Societies* (Thousand Oaks, CA: Sage Publications, Inc., 2004), 669–719. In the GLOBE project, 170 social scientists from around the world investigated the relationships between societal culture, organizational culture, leadership, and organizational effectiveness. Data were gathered from about 17,000 middle managers in 951 organizations across three industries in 62 countries
6. M. Dalton, C. Ernst, J. Deal, & J. Leslie, *Success for the New Global Manager* (San Francisco: Jossey-Bass, A Wiley Company, 2002).
7. D. Pattnaik, *Don't Stop that Babbling*. Available at http://devdutt.com/don%E2%80%99t-stop-that-babbling.

7

TWO FUNDAMENTAL EXPERIENCES FOR NEW MANAGERS

Experiences at work are powerful transmitters of leadership lessons. For example, even senior managers learn to lead more effectively from horizontal moves or crossing cultures. But two additional kinds of experiences stand out because of their impact on early- and midcareer managers. These are an increase in job scope from a promotion; and the manager's first professional job. In our research, each was highlighted by at least one in four of the interviewed executives.

The lessons mined from such experiences are highly important because they occur during a formative phase of managerial careers. Joining an organization and being promoted are important life transitions, especially in India. Unlike people in the U.S. and other Western countries, young Indians do not hold jobs during high school or college—joining an organization brings them their first work experience. Moreover, "doing well" at work, as validated by promotions, confers considerable satisfaction and social standing on them and their families.

There are also cultural traditions demarcating the four stages, or *ashrams*, of life as that of a student, householder, retiree, and ascetic (or the *brahmacharya*, *grahasta*, *vanaprastha*, and *sanyasa ashrams*). Each entails specific and different obligations. A student studies and a householder earns a living and manages a household. (As an aside, the obligations of the retiree include social welfare; and that of the ascetic is to seek spiritual fulfillment as a recluse; but these two stages are not relevant to this discussion.) Norms for the *brahmachari* and *grahasthi* may change in the future but are accepted to date. Signing on to one's first job is linked to crossing over into adulthood. Research confirms that when making a transition, individuals become more "ready to learn."[1] No wonder then that young managers are eager to learn all they can about their job and about leadership.

Job scope increases are discussed first because of the traditionally important lessons learned, in comparison with first professional jobs, which convey more personal and nuanced lessons. From job scope increases, managers who until then have been handling lower levels of responsibility and complexity, advance their functional and technical expertise and learn to manage and motivate subordinates. From first professional jobs, a niche experience in the manager's personal growth journey, impressions about leadership are gathered and personal leadership insights are formed.

Leadership lessons are learned in several ways (see chapter 1, table 1.1). In this chapter, we focus on *functional and technical expertise* and its relevance to leader effectiveness. And though "first jobs" are part of the past and not the future for most readers, we take you back in time to the first stage of your career to unearth valuable nuggets of *personal leadership insights*.

INCREASE IN JOB SCOPE

Many managers climb career ladders quickly during their early or middle stages of work life. Their vertical rise takes them to new roles with bigger budgets, more people to be managed, and greater access to resources. Their range of accountabilities expands, and the pressures to perform become far more intense. The promoted manager's successes and failures are more visible to others within and outside the organization.

Over the past couple of decades in India, a leap in job scope has been triggered by fantastic domestic growth and the internationalization of business. Senior managers' outstanding performance or strenuous efforts to grow the business domestically or internationally are recognized by top management; and they are rewarded by being given significantly greater accountabilities. In turn, bottom-line responsibility is handed over for the first time to mid- and junior-level managers. For example, a midlevel manager is promoted to branch manager or head of a profit center or function head. Younger employees then move upward to take on their first supervisory assignment.

The small jumps in scope at junior and middle levels do not place managers in the rarefied atmosphere at the top of an organization. But in effect, each step up on the lower rungs of the ladder also brings more responsibilities and visibility. The impact on the manager's development as a leader is inevitable, primarily because they come at a time when they are still learning the ropes of leadership.

Reactions to increases in job scope are captured next, reflecting the performance pressures that managers must bear. The remarks inform us of their developmental needs—for functional and technical knowledge to face expanded roles and better interpersonal skills to work with subordinates.

In the Hot Seat

The sprinkling of comments that follow portray the feelings of the promoted manager. They range from awe at the immense span of responsibilities that have landed on them at a young age, to ambivalence about having experts and elders reporting to them, to concern about running a function about which they know very little, to gratitude for the services they can give others.

- So, imagine this situation. I'm 34. I'm an Indian CEO, and I've been given this huge responsibility—the budgets are bigger, and it's on a much wider scale. The whole complexity is much bigger.

- The engineer-in-charge resigned. He submitted his resignation in the morning, and in the afternoon he walked out. Suddenly, in addition to my projects, I had 35 qualified engineers reporting to me who were experts in their field. I didn't know anything about them or about engineering. I didn't know how the boiler worked; I didn't know how the electricity supplies were controlled; I knew nothing.
- I was three years old in the company. I was still raw and that's when my factory manager gave me a responsibility to handle, which overnight doubled my area of operation and gave me a far bigger chunk of the factory operation. Traditionally, this would have been handled by two people. But he just combined the responsibilities and asked me to handle them.
- From sales, I became the head of a company unit. Here, there was a different learning. I needed to attend board meetings, talk to directors, and a whole lot of things. That was a little intimidating and a little frightening in the beginning.
- I was given charge of the chairmanship. I only had to follow the mandate of the board. That is when I felt that a God-sent opportunity had been given to me for uplifting the poorest of the poor people.

Whether promotions move managers into the middle, senior, or top levels of their organization, the increased job scope presses on them to shore up their efficiency and productivity, master new areas of expertise, and become profit driven, as illustrated in the story that follows.

A Profitable Learning

Mr. Ranjan had passed out of a northern Indian university as a chemical engineer. Upon graduation, he joined a leading

Indian packaging company as a trainee. He was given charge of front-line sales, and product and market development. Over 17 years, he moved from one major Indian city to another, living and working in Kolkata, Mumbai, Indore, and Chennai. Gradually, his regional marketing responsibilities were increased. A significant opportunity came his way when he was asked to head the all-India marketing of packaging products and run a profit center as a business head.

This highly visible increase in his responsibilities was not a surprise to Mr. Ranjan or his colleagues. He had a history of successfully contributing to the domestic and international growth of his company. Early in his career, he had personally contacted the distributors of its milk cartons in the mid-East and quadrupled total export sales from one-quarter of a million to one million cartons annually. He achieved this by offering good prices, on-time delivery, and timely collection of money owed. He had enjoyed a similar string of small successes in his various regional assignments.

Given his significant promotion to all-India business head, Mr. Ranjan earnestly took on the diversification of his company's packaging products. For the first time, he encountered complications from working with subcontractors running small-scale businesses. That is when he first learned important lessons about profitability.

"That appointment gave me an insight about what profitability and cash flow is all about," he said.

> We had to look at the suppliers of raw materials, and then work with vendors. We looked at current specs, alternate specs, and new-generation specs. We thought over and over again about how to give value addition to our customers and have them stick to us for a long time. This was not about short-term action and reducing prices for a year. At the end of the think, we were able to hold vendors responsible for quality, quantity, and therefore profitability. That was my first step in moving from hardcore marketing to profit center management.

In the forthcoming section on lessons to learn, we discuss the central importance of new functional and technical knowledge, such as that acquired by Mr. Ranjan, to effective leadership.

FIRST PROFESSIONAL JOB: ADJUSTING TO THE WORLD OF WORK

The freshly minted managers are exposed, for the first time, to life in an organization and to the demands of a professional career. Why is this experience important to their development as leaders? As they step onto the first rung of the career ladder, they learn about the world of work and have to adjust; and several encounter situations that clarify their personal leadership insights and teach them what integrity means.

When the Going Gets Tough

A surprise, and sometimes a shock, looms before the young man or woman who has just graduated with a degree. She is leaving behind her world of books, learning projects, and friendly rivalry from classmates and plunging into the abrupt, frantic, and relentless interactions of the workplace. As told by some interviewees, they were taken aback by what they faced on their first job! Each encountered situations that did not meet their expectations.

- The initial glamour of joining a world-renowned organization was quickly replaced by the drudgery of daily routine. "The brand is the only thing that is glamorous about this company," said Harish, remembering his first job in a beverage distributorship. He found himself working from 7 a.m. to midnight, managing warehouse space for stock coming in and going out. He learned to adjust. He taught himself to drive a truck to win over the illiterate drivers who doubled as delivery staff and salespeople.

- Academically gifted and a state-ranked graduate, Ram was selected to report directly to the chairman of the bank. Looking back, he described how at 22, he was inclined to think of himself as "God's gift to mankind." He had peremptorily dropped off an important memorandum from the chairman's office with the telefax operator. Two days later, the message had still not gone out. By then, Ram had taken the trouble to learn the telefax operator's name. He asked: "Biren, what happened? How come this hasn't gone? It's from the chairman's office!" Giving him an inscrutable look, Biren pointed to the stack of memos on his desk and answered, "You see all these other messages here? They're all from the chairman's office." In retrospect, Ram laughed ruefully: "How could I go to the chairman and say to him that the telefax operator would not listen to me?" Ram learned that his credentials did not automatically earn him authority or respect, but that showing respect created cooperation.
- The assignment that Girish was promised when he was recruited never materialized. He found that in the five months that lapsed between the job interview and him joining the company, the business environment had turned sour, the company's finances were faltering, its strategic priorities had shifted, and the job for which he had been hired was eliminated. Born and brought up in Maharashtra, and expecting to work there, he was shunted to a small office in Kolkata and assigned to corporate finance. The situation felt like a triple setback to him—moving to an unfamiliar region of the country, without a social network, and in a function about which he knew nothing. On looking back though, this appointment turned out to be one of the most interesting nine-month periods in his life.

He learned to make a new circle of friends. His newfound friends even helped him adjust to a new location and to work life.

Some jobseekers are recruited by a small company of which they have never heard before; but their assignment turns out to be perfectly suited to their interests, skills, and passions. Others are completely surprised by the privilege of being selected for training outside India and the preparations they must make to leave their home country for the first time. What many graduates learn to do is assimilate new perspectives and adjust expectations. This flexibility serves them well in their future years as managers.

FIRST PROFESSIONAL JOB: REAPING LEADERSHIP INSIGHTS

What does it take to be effective as a leader? The question is perennial, and comes up throughout the manager's career. By reflecting on this, managers form personal working rules about how to lead and manage successfully. There are many examples of the principles that they formulate for themselves over time, concerning, for example, the importance of perseverance, desired behaviors toward subordinates, handling crises, the need for optimism, responding to success and failure, and much else. But the first harvest of impressions about leadership comes from the manager's first few seasons of work.

Among various insights about leadership, one in five executives discussed how they had come to value integrity. For many, their commitment to act with integrity was learned during their first work experience or in early life. The *Random House Dictionary of the English Language*[2] lists three meanings for "integrity":

1. soundness of and adherence to moral principle and character; uprightness; honesty.

2. the state of being whole, entire, or undiminished.
3. a sound, unimpaired, or perfect condition.

In our interviews, the meaning of "integrity" accords with the first two definitions, and is exemplified by courage and honesty shown in publicly expressed words and actions.

Courage and honesty: in practice, these translate into a conscious choice on the part of the managers to speak or act in keeping with personal principles, perspectives, and beliefs. This is despite the possibility of negative consequences to themselves. But if the consequences of talking and acting with integrity are positive, especially for managers on their first job, their confidence levels climb too.

Integrity arises in situations where young managers are called on to protect the interests of their company or coworkers. Integrity also means speaking up to prevent unfairness to oneself or conducting business with reference to the company's code of conduct. All these circumstances call for courage and honesty.

Peter Drucker, a prodigious thinker and writer on management, regarded "integrity" as the touchstone of management.[3] He remarked: "The people with whom a person works, and especially subordinates, know in a few weeks whether he or she [a manager] has integrity or not. They may forgive a person for a great deal; incompetence, ignorance, insecurity, or bad manners. But they will not forgive a lack of integrity in that person."[4]

Personal integrity radiates genuineness. The leader's integrity is crucial for creating trusting relationships in a business world that is a minefield of temptations to be expedient, self-serving, and unethical. We share the following examples from the interview data about how young managers learned to value integrity in themselves.

Fair Play

On his first assignment as a trainee, and while on probation, Anand Mansukhani was given sales responsibility for home furniture for five states in northwestern India. One of the distributors—an elderly and respected gentleman—was a close friend of his company's owner and also a senior politician in the central government. But his dealership was being mismanaged by his son-in-law. Since the son-in-law's poor management practices were causing Anand's company to lose market share, Anand decided to issue a couple of warnings and then find another distributor.

Of course, word of his intent reached the company's owner, who asked his managing director to follow up with a visit to the distributorship. All Anand's peers were alarmed. They had warned him earlier that stringent oversight was not a part of their company culture. With the owner's personal involvement, they felt sure that for Anand, trouble lay ahead.

But the managing director surprised everyone with his handling of the situation. He cleverly balanced everybody's best interests and that of their company too. Anand was given an opportunity to make the business case for his proposal. Then the MD met privately with the owner's elderly friend, and assured him that their company would give him full support for meeting his sales volume. He also authorized Anand to appoint a different distributor and open a new dealership in the same city.

Anand, of course, was overjoyed that his company upheld fair business practices despite personal loyalties stemming from friendships. His commitment to protecting the interests of his company had paid off. He learned that he wanted his actions to accord with his beliefs, and was pleased that he was working for a company in which his integrity was respected. Mostly, his honesty and courage in sticking to his business instincts were supported by his superiors, which reinforced his resolve to be a person of integrity.

Protecting the Company's Interests

Young managers show integrity when they deal with vendors with transparency and fairness. They do this by analyzing business issues objectively. Their cross-examination of stakeholders is thorough. They strive to make impartial decisions. Most of all, they show courage by taking positions that run counter to popular opinion when necessary.

The payoff is in the trust that is eventually vested in them by their associates and all who do business with them, and of course, in the cascading effect of their integrity on subordinates who emulate them. This is how Aninda Pandey and P. K. Krishnamurty handled their business dilemmas, noting what they gained as a result.

- Aninda Pandey got posted to eastern Uttar Pradesh as an area sales manager for agricultural products. Aninda discovered that the dealers were hoarding products to drive up prices. They had the previous year's stock sitting in their warehouses unsold, but wanted to be supplied with the current year's stock. Though the dealers insisted that they had done their best to sell the previous year's stock, Aninda was not convinced. His informal market survey told him that demand for the product was high and the previous year's stock could be sold. Since his company would suffer financial losses if the previous year's stock was not marketed, he informed the dealers that they would not get new stock until the old stock was sold. Switching their ploy, the dealers agreed to sell previous stock, but negotiated hard to get new stock too. Aninda would not budge. He stuck to his decision to withhold new stock until the old was sold. According to Aninda, the dealers eventually cooperated with him because he was willing to confront them and to engage in weeks of honest exchanges of information. "It was a great lesson for me that if you are fair and transparent, and people are able to see that, they will generally come with you and they will not then resist." He noted that this early work experience helped him establish that he would not be pushed around, knew what he was doing, and was able to deliver and not just talk. This strengthened Aninda's belief in dealing with issues head on, with courage and honesty.

- As a 22-year-old, P. K. Krishnamurty's initial assignment was to a hostile, backward rural area in Andhra Pradesh, where none of his predecessors had succeeded in establishing a trading post for crops. Since he was from that region and spoke the regional language, company leaders hoped he could turn the situation around. But they warned him that he would most likely fail and lose his job. P. K. found that in his dealings with the villagers, he had to steer a middle course between taking risks and protecting his company's investment. Every day required exercising judgment and making difficult decisions. What served him best, in his opinion, was that he was honest and treated the villagers as equals. As they grew to like and trust him, they stopped being obstructive, and began to cooperate with his efforts to establish the outpost. This experience set the tone for P. K.'s future leadership style of being honest, respectful, fair, and firm.

Protecting Colleagues

When colleagues were treated unfairly, Mr. Ramachandran and Aparna did not look the other way. They stepped forward to take whatever actions they could.

- V. Ramachandran graduated with engineering and business management degrees from prestigious Indian universities, and then joined an advertising agency. During his second year, his agency won the bid to design a brand-building campaign for a leading U.K.-based multinational. The project team had barely started work when V. Ramachandran observed that a young, promising new hire with innovative solutions was suppressed and maligned by the senior team members—within the company and to the client. Mr. Ramachandran felt that the new employee was being treated unfairly by individuals who were selfishly protecting their own interests. He pulled out all the stops to ensure that his bosses learned of the situation and maneuvered to protect the young man from veiled and false criticisms that would jeopardize his career.

The advertising campaign successfully improved the client's brand image; and the young man continued to deliver on building key brands. From this incident, Mr. Ramachandran began to believe that managers should assume responsibility for exposing the Machiavellian tactics of other managers, who protect their own selfish interests while harming others. He became more committed than before to principled and rational behaviors that would be fair to employees and improve productivity.

- Aparna Chowdury was in the second year of her first job with a bank. Her small team was responsible for structuring finance projects. One unfortunate day, she saw a younger colleague publicly humiliated by a senior professional from their department. She knew that the senior colleague was under pressure to book more deals and ratchet up business volumes; but the incident rankled. She was upset and asked for a transfer, informing her business head that she did not wish to work in a department that condoned such behavior. Her boss warned Aparna about her career-limiting attitude, since employees did not get to choose their placement. Aparna requested, and was given, a day off.

  The next day brought a surprise. She was escorted to meet with the deputy managing director, who understood her position, was willing to investigate the senior manager's transgression, and gave Aparna the choice of moving to another group after a two-week break. When Aparna returned, she joined another group. She was gratified that her feelings mattered and that her concerns were met. Though she did not directly confront her senior colleague and chose to change workgroups, the incident taught her the importance of speaking up to express her values.

Once again, we note Drucker's enduring assertion: when leaders mean what they say, that is integrity of character, and their spirit of integrity permeates the organization. Drucker strongly believed that personal integrity had to be a part of everything a leader did; without that, leaders would not have legitimacy, and their followers would eventually desert them.[5]

LESSON 10: FUNCTIONAL AND TECHNICAL EXPERTISE

Among all leadership lessons, functional and technical expertise is one that is traditionally valued and formally taught through courses for baccalaureate and master's degrees and specialized programs. For professional credibility, all leaders need such expertise as a starting point. But successful executives continue to broaden and deepen their core knowledge throughout their careers.

This occurs from ongoing experiences, for example, due to a promotion and increased job scope. New initiatives and horizontal moves also increase expertise. These three types of experiences in particular produce new knowledge about different aspects of running a business, such as accounting and finance, e-business, operations, marketing communication, HR systems, and so forth. In-depth technical knowledge about the company's processes, products, and services advances too.

As they progress through the ranks, the relevance of the leader's expertise seemingly recedes to the background, and social intelligence and business acumen come to center stage. But today, with innovative communication technologies exploding on the scene and new knowledge growing exponentially, "expertise" continues to be at the core of running businesses successfully. In the final analysis, expertise gives leaders the edge on staying abreast of breaking innovations and on positioning their business for continuing success.

Step 1: Pause and Reflect

Without doubt, functional and technical credentials are a prerequisite for entry-level managers. What this research highlights is the continual need to build on that foundational knowledge. The behaviors in table 7.1 help you to assess your disposition to do so.

Step 2: Assess Yourself

Using the scale of 1 to 5 (with 1 = Never, 2 = Occasionally, 3 = Often, 4 = Usually, and 5 = Always), rate yourself on how often you practice the four behaviors in table 7.1. As you respond, consider whether your boss and peers would agree with the ratings that you are giving yourself. Keeping this in

Table 7.1 Assessment: Functional and technical expertise

Behavior	*Self-rating*
Learning new technical or functional knowledge quickly	
Interpreting statistics, graphs, charts, and accounting statements proficiently	
Taking interest in the work of different functional groups	
Seeking a broad range of business knowledge and skills	

mind, come up with your final ratings. This will give you a picture of your potential for increasing your expertise.

Step 3: Take Action

You are undoubtedly already technically and functionally proficient. But how can you plan to maintain and expand what you know? One approach is to stay informed about available executive education and training programs. Many business organizations have departments that maintain an inventory of resources that focus on developing managers' knowledge and skills. You can also find resources on your own or create your own opportunities for learning. For example, you could take on a short assignment in a different functional group; or substitute for a colleague who is on leave; or ask for a job rotation; or develop and deliver a workshop for your team about the work of a different function.

There are many different ways in which managers can push the limits of what they know about their business and profession. Even short social conversations with co-workers and friends can open up new possibilities to pursue.

LESSON 11: PERSONAL LEADERSHIP INSIGHTS

Managers whose portfolio includes the first six experiences that have already been described are well on their way to becoming successful senior leaders. They have learned much from bosses, improved profitability in fix-it and turnaround situations, created new business initiatives, transitioned through horizontal moves, worked in a different culture or cultures, and survived and thrived with greatly expanded scopes of responsibility. Their experiences have been the portal to a treasure trove of leadership lessons. They are more confident and self-aware, and have learned to manage, motivate, and develop subordinates. They can work through the politics of their company, influence others, and engage in an effective manner with stakeholders inside and outside their organization. By practicing adaptability, they have gained cross-cultural savvy. With their all-round expertise, and capacity for effective execution, innovation, and entrepreneurship, these managers are a rich asset to any company.

Yet it benefits even exceptionally well-qualified managers to reminisce about their early work experiences and lessons learned. Rewinding to a time when they watched and listened to others, especially bosses and superiors, brings recollections of waking up to the meaning of leadership and integrity. As young managers, they collected impressions and formed beliefs about which leadership abilities are the most important, how leaders should act in different situations, and what values leaders should display. Like a seed below ground, their personal leadership insights germinated in the fertile soil of early professional jobs. Fast-forwarding to the present, the ideas about leadership that subliminally captured managers' imaginations many years earlier continue to guide what they say and do as leaders later in their careers.

Step 1: Pause and Reflect

Think back to your first work experience. What did you learn about the world of work? What rules were you expected to follow? Whom did you turn to for guidance and why did you select that person? What guidance did he or she give you? Were there people who inspired you and whom you decided to emulate? What did you learn from them about management and leadership? How have you incorporated your learning into the way you behave as a leader?

Having given these questions some thought, find a listener who is sincerely interested in hearing about your first job experience. Even better, find someone who wants to talk about his or her experience and listen to yours. Start by exchanging the memories stimulated by a few of the questions above.

Next, ask each other the following controversial questions to pull up deeper insights. Were there situations where you called to question the wisdom of what was said and done? Or incidents that went against your principles or feelings about what is "right"? What happened and how did you react? Did you discuss the situation? If yes, with whom? What course of action did you follow? Looking back, are you satisfied with what you did? If you could travel back in time and relive those circumstances, what would you say or do differently?

To conclude, take time to reflect and ask yourself: what does this exercise tell you about your own leadership commitments? To what extent are honesty and courage a part of your style of leading? More important, are you pleased about who you are as a leader, the choices you make, and what this says about your integrity? Or are you interested in polishing these facets of yourself? And how do you continuously deepen your insights about leadership?

Step 2: Assess Yourself

Using the scale of 1 to 5 (with 1 = Never, 2 = Occasionally, 3 = Often, 4 = Usually, and 5 = Always), rate yourself on the seven practices in table 7.2. How often have you follow each

Table 7.2 Assessment: Personal leadership insights

Behavior	*Self-rating*
Having a personal philosophy about leadership	
Committing to improving my ability to lead	
Taking responsibility for aligning my behavior with my values	
Communicating honestly when working with others	
Following through on unpopular but necessary actions	
Persevering in the face of obstacles and criticism	
Displaying a distinctive and positive style of leading	

practice? As you respond, consider whether others who know you well would agree with the ratings that you are giving yourself. Keeping this in mind, come up with your final ratings. This process will stimulate you to deepen your personal insights about, and commitment to, leading effectively.

Step 3: Take Action

Managers have to make profoundly personal choices to shape their leadership commitments. Like a stone thrown into a pond, their choices ripple into circles of influence on people and the culture of their workplace. Given the intimate conversations that managers must have with themselves to first deepen their insights about leadership, the action that makes the most sense is further reflection. The salient questions to reflect on are: what is the practical value of having a personal approach to leadership? In the past, in what ways have you shown courage or honesty as a manager and what were the consequences? What values concerning work and relationships with people do you most want to display through your own style of leading? Finally, how do your reflections illuminate the next steps on your pathway to effective leadership?

IMPLICATIONS FOR INDIAN MANAGERS

The experiences described in this chapter introduce early career managers to the basics of leadership: *functional and technical expertise* and *personal leadership insights*. Youngsters go to school first to learn the alphabet, and then to read, which opens their minds to more learning and knowledge. From first job experiences, and promotions that increase job scope, managers learn the alphabet of leadership and start to read the language of managerial assignments. This literacy about organizational work equips them to learn from other experiences that follow.

Early career experiences—such as first professional jobs, increases in job scope, and other assignments in the first stages of work life—afford a once-in-a-lifetime learning opportunity to tomorrow's upcoming business leaders. They are transitioning into adult roles, and their own patterns of thinking and acting are not entrenched. The pressures to prove themselves and succeed increase receptivity and speed up new learning. Initial experiences and lessons learned become a platform for reaching for further experiences and lessons.

These comments are also pertinent to those who are accountable for the throughput in leadership talent pipelines. How a new batch of managers, or managers who are transitioning into new responsibilities, are habituated to learn from experiences inculcates their personal methodology for how to go about subsequent learning.

Why is this important? Earlier, I compared a child learning the alphabet and reading with a young adult learning the fundamental skills of leadership. Now, with the help of Alvin Toffler, I add a twist to the meaning of literacy. This futurist reminds us that "the illiterate of the 21st century will not be those who cannot read and write, but those who cannot learn, unlearn, and relearn."[6] This point is subtle and vital—early career years are important for all of us not only due to what we learn, but also due to how we learn to learn. This overarching theme is the focus of the final chapter.

ENDNOTES

1. W. Bridges, *Managing Transitions: Making the Most of Change* (Philadelphia: Perseus Books Group, 2009); W. C. Musselwhite, *The Impact of Timing on Readiness to Learn and Transfer of Learning from Leadership Development Training: A Case Study* [dissertation] (Raleigh, NC: North Carolina State University, 1985). Available from: Dissertation Abstracts International at http://www.essaytown.com/writing/dissertation-abstracts-international.

2. J. Stein (editor in chief), *The Random House Dictionary of the English Language: The Unabridged Edition* (New York, NY: Random House, 1967).
3. J. A. Maciariello, The Importance of Integrity in a Leader and Personal Relationships. *Leader to Leader*, 2010; S1:43–6.
4. P. F. Drucker, *The Daily Drucker: 366 Days of Insight and Motivation for Getting the Right Things Done* (New York, NY: HarperCollins Publishers, Inc., 2004).
5. W. A. Cohen, *Drucker on Leadership: New Lessons from the Father of Modern Management* (San Francisco: Jossey-Bass, 2010).
6. A. Toffler, *Quotations about Learning*. Available at: http://www.quotegarden.com/learning.html.

8

HARNESSING THE POWER OF EXPERIENCE

> You can't connect the dots looking forward; you can only connect them looking backwards. So you have to trust that the dots will somehow connect in your future. You have to trust in something—your gut, destiny, life, karma, whatever. This approach has never let me down, and it has made all the difference in my life.
>
> —*Steve Jobs, CEO, Apple Computer, and Pixar Animation Studios*[1]

Steve Jobs expresses feelings that are familiar to most of us: each life is lived looking forward, but its meaning only comes by looking backward. "Seven experiences, 11 lessons" proposes that young managers become forward looking and design their managerial career, to the extent possible. This advantage comes from the willingness of contemporary senior leaders to look backward and share their memories, which have been culled into the themes and stories in this book; and these can be used to project forward.

Whatever you call your endeavors—harvesting experiences, climbing a ladder of experience, assembling a portfolio of experiences, putting together a jigsaw puzzle with pieces of experience, seeking a spectrum of experience, or connecting your dots of experience—we suggest you devise an image or metaphor. The point is to pursue work experiences and the leadership lessons learned through experiences avidly; a personally meaningful metaphor or vivid image can spur you to do so.

Many examples have been given of dedicated, passionate, and talented managers who have taught themselves to become ever more effective as leaders. As a reader, if you are now motivated and ready to embark proactively on your own development, or give impetus to the development of others under your wing, we provide a simple model: *the Learning-to-Learn Equation* (see figure 8.1).[2] This model is popularly used in programs and modules offered by the CCL. In this chapter, the model has been adapted to direct your attention to four concluding action-oriented tips that round off what you now know about leader development. To my best knowledge, these are the last pieces of the puzzle of becoming a leader. The tips address how you can:

- gauge your motivation and readiness to learn
- nurture your ability to learn
- engage with experiences, and build and broaden the lessons you learn
- use your leadership lessons to benefit yourself, others, your organization, and society.

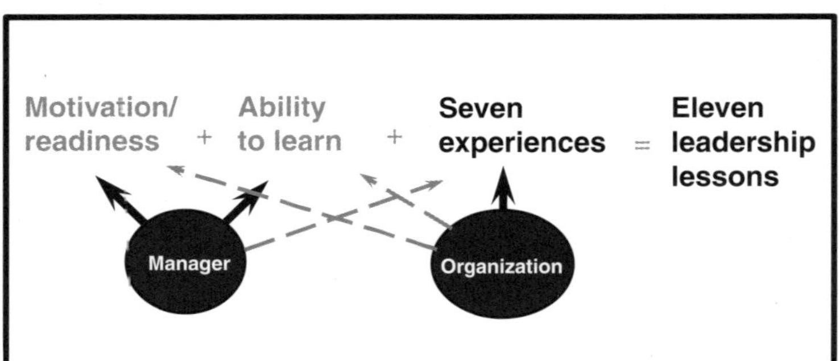

Figure 8.1 The Learning-to-Learn Equation

The figure shows that learning from experiences is a process in which the manager and his or her organization participate. As indicated by the solid arrows, the manager is the primary source of *motivation or readiness* and *ability to learn*, while the organization is the primary source of *experiences*. The broken-line arrows signify where the manager and the organization each have a secondary influence. In this model, the three elements on the left sum to the leadership lessons on the right.

GAUGING MOTIVATION AND READINESS

Here is a riddle that has not been solved: given the same powerful experience, why do some managers learn while others do not? Experiences do not guarantee that a manager will become a successful leader.[3] Though the manager's career is dotted with experiences, learning from them is not automatic. "Experience is not what happens to a man, it is what a man does with what happens to him," observed Aldous Huxley.[4] If so, the question that begs to be asked is: how are individuals different in their motivation and readiness to learn from experience?

We portray Udaharan, a consummate learner, as an exemplar with whom you can compare yourself. His orientation to learning is ideal. *Learning orientation* is a pattern of preferences for facing unknown circumstances and its discomforts. *Learning orientation* is a mirror of beliefs about personal growth and development. Note that the important question of what prompts you to learn from novel circumstances is left for you to answer.

The fictitious Udaharan is an up-and-coming manager in his mid-30s. He works for an Indian multinational company in the hospitality industry. Udaharan *takes advantage of opportunities* to do something new, and treats all situations as a chance to learn something. To others, his motto seems to be: learn everything you can, any time you can, from anyone you can—there will always come a time when you will be grateful you did![5] Admired because he *asks perceptive questions*, Udaharan *has a track record of improving knowledge and skills* in the seven years since he joined his company.

When placed in unfamiliar situations, Udaharan *tries to understand others' perspectives*. He *listens well*, and does not typically assume that he is the one with the best solutions. Since he does not let power or status go to his head, he *creates good give-and-take* with others in a conversation or meeting. By taking in ideas that are different from his, he can be *flexible in responding to situations* and moderates what he says and the course of action that he takes up. He is effective at working through most job-related issues.

In his mid-20s, Udaharan was fortunate to enroll in a leadership development program for young managers. That was a life-changing event that accentuated his learning orientation. During this program, he learned to *value feedback* from others and do self-reflection. He began to ask co-workers discreetly about the impression he was making and the impact on them of what he said and did as a manager. He also started to *keep a journal*, teaching himself to audit his job assignments. When working on a project, he would stop from time to time to consider whether he was achieving necessary results. Udaharan would turn over in his mind what was working or not, and think about what he needed to keep doing, stop doing, and do differently. He would *set goals* and plan the changes that he needed to make in his handling of the assignment and then *follow up on his plan*.

Over the years, Udaharan came to understand why it is important to *show humility*. He could see that when others observe that their manager acknowledges personal limitations, is not easily offended by criticism, and is willing to change, they are honest with him or her. Though this has not been easy to put into practice, Udaharan now knows that unless he learns to own his shortcomings, he will not get the cooperation he needs from others to compensate for his weak points as a leader and manager. Nor will he achieve the goals of his organization.

Udaharan is a composite of all the attitudes and behaviors that make up a terrific orientation to learning. Like the digitally constructed picture of an ideally handsome man or beautiful woman, he contains all the elements of a perfectly learning-oriented manager. This portrait of Udaharan, which is compiled from the results of fine-grained psychometric analysis,[6] is meant to rouse you to ponder your own learning orientation. A proper learning orientation is so essential to successful leadership today that estimating one's qualities as a learner, rather than as a leader, is much more pertinent to career progress.

But a learning orientation is just one part of the action. Even Udaharan needs to flex between learning tactics, which are described next.

NURTURING ABILITY TO LEARN

Managers can consciously use experiences to create new learning within themselves.[7] Self-development is a dynamic process of unlearning and relearning—letting go of old views and behaviors, and taking on new habits of thinking and acting that redress the problematic situation at hand more effectively. But mindset change is a glacially slow process.

Mindset changes become possible when the manager has to cope with unfamiliar circumstances, but does not succumb to tension and stress. (Managing tension is critical, and this point will be re-emphasized shortly.) Instead, by ruminating by themselves and with others, and experimenting with alternate angles of thought, the manager and his or her team become penetratingly perceptive about their situation. Their perceptual shift is the source of shifts in thoughts, words, and deeds, contributing to improved performance and greater leadership effectiveness. Two narratives are examples of such a shift in a mid- and top-level team respectively: Rajgopal's story of "Beating the Odds" in chapter 3; and Kumarji's story of "Innovation Multiplied: One Stop Shops in Rural India" in chapter 4.

According to the Center's research, which builds on the work of David Kolb,[8] superior learners blend four learning tactics (see table 8.1); and like Udaharan, they tend to seek out both challenges and feedback from their environment.[9] By learning tactics, we mean the basics of thinking, accessing others, taking action, and staying in touch with feelings, which is how effective managers forge through any circumstance that they encounter for the first time. Table 8.1 is a

Table 8.1 Four learning tactics

Learning tactic	*What the manager prefers*	*What the manager does*
Feeling	To reflect on feelings, emotions and attitudes about how the problem affects him or her	Manages anxiety and uncertainty associated with new and difficult undertakings Acknowledges the impact of feelings on himself or herself Trusts his or her gut instincts Confronts him- or herself when avoidance behaviors are recognized
Thinking	To reflect and work alone to plan, strategize, and envision	Recalls the past for similar or contrasting situations Imagines the future and plays out possibilities in his or her mind's eye Gathers information from books and reports to get the facts
Accessing others	To gain assistance and support to solve problems and learn	Seeks advice, support or instruction from people who have met a similar challenge Learns by watching someone else Takes a relevant course or program
Taking action	To act on the problem, get resolution, reduce stress, and learn	Learns by doing Uses a hands-on approach to tackling a challenge in real time Figures it out as he or she goes along

useful overview of the tactics with simple descriptions of what managers prefer and do. Unfortunately, there is the human tendency to over-rely habitually on one or two favored tactics, which is not effective. Again, we leave it to you to investigate and discover whether you use all four learning tactics in a balanced way.

When it comes to learning to learn (or learning how to learn), there is one high hurdle that has to be jumped. That high hurdle is the stress or tension from meeting unfamiliar and sometimes worrisome circumstances. In table 8.1, surmounting this hurdle is described as "manages anxiety and uncertainty associated with new and difficult undertakings."

Psychological research tells us that adult personalities evolve by working their way through the stress of new situations. "Stress," as used in this context, is the stimulus that disturbs or interferes with the normal physiological equilibrium of an organism.[10] Coping with stress is a continual internal process, and sustaining internal equilibrium is prerequisite for managers who wish to make the most of their experiences and develop themselves. In chapter 3, Alam Kapur, Mr. Mehra, and Mr. Chandrasekar are all examples of managers who were pummeled by stress (over which they prevailed) into becoming stronger, more relentless and, paradoxically, more humane as leaders.

Managers' habitual reactions to stress are thus enormously significant. Controlling internally experienced stress levels is like setting a thermostat to regulate temperature. In other words, by regulating their experience of stress, managers create a climate within themselves for sustaining personal growth. I offer two more perspectives, the first based on research and the second on my personal views.

Studies by behavioral scientists tell us that when managers are faced with a demanding task, they consciously or unconsciously appraise the situation: does the challenge threaten their personal wellbeing? Will they be able to deal with what is in front of them?[11] Those who surmount self-defeating thoughts and emotions, and focus on the task at hand function better and learn more.[12]

An issue that continues to intrigue me is how stress can be contained and channeled so that the manager's energy is used productively, not dissipated or wasted. My musings turn toward the battlefield of Kurukshetra, where Prince Arjuna agonized over his dilemma of having to go to war with his relatives, beloved friends, and teachers. This is where Krishna, his divine charioteer, counseled the tense and overwhelmed prince. Lord Krishna's words are the heart of the *Bhagavad Gita*—a scriptural, literary, and philosophical text to which contemporary Indian managers often turn for moral guidance.

To aid Arjuna to overcome his fears, hesitation, and bewilderment, Krishna speaks to him about fulfilling his *dharma*, or duty, without attaching himself to the fruit or outcomes of his actions. To this struggling human soul, Krishna conveys a timeless teaching about dealing with ordeals—by not being swayed by the "fruits of action" or thoughts of success or failure, maintaining equanimity or even-mindedness, and engaging in dutiful action.

My reasoning is by no means scholarly. I have been perplexed by Lord Krishna's injunction that seems to me to contravene the focus on "outcomes" demanded of business leaders. I have come to believe that Krishna's message to Arjuna is shaded not just by the morality of curbing expectations and attachment to outcomes, but also by the pragmatic need to help Arjuna fulfill his leadership role, without succumbing to stress from preoccupation with outcomes.

This reflection on the central message of the *Bhagavad Gita* is not a detour. The preceding sections aim to clarify the learning orientation and learning tactics that can best aid Indian managers to become leaders; and learning to quell feelings of stress ("*karm karo, phal ki chinta mat karo*") is a crucial aspect. Having explored how motivation and ability to learn are relevant to becoming a leader, we outline two ways of becoming more effective: building skills for leadership mastery; and broadening skills for leadership versatility.

BUILD AND BROADEN: ENGAGING WITH EXPERIENCES

New learning includes becoming more proficient at existing skills (by building) *and* developing new skills (by broadening). Whatever assignments lie ahead, they can be used to build or broaden leadership skill or both.[13] But what should your immediate next step be—to build or broaden? For readers who have worked through the exercises in earlier chapters and formed their growth goals, this is the moment for a reality check. Your organization's growth goals, for the business and for you, now enter the picture.

How is your organization positioning itself for future growth? This could be, for example, by expanding to new geographical territories in India, company acquisitions, market segmentation to diversify customer base, internationalization, outsourcing, new product development, or some combination of these. Each growth strategy calls on second- and third-tier managers to prepare for leadership, but in different ways. You may be able to decipher which leadership abilities and behaviors are highly regarded by observing how your organization's top-tier leaders are shuffled and repositioned. For example, in the repositioning, is technical expertise or marketing expertise emphasized more? Is a manager's solo creation of a vision admired more than his or her ability to motivate a team? If your company's strategic priorities and desired competencies are not sufficiently clear to you, then it makes sense to check with a superior about how you need to develop yourself.

Asking how you can upgrade yourself is a reliable starting point for a conversation with a boss. He or she can inform you about what he or she sees as your talents and where he or she sees potential for improvement. The payoff comes from jointly determining which one or two improvements you can make in the near future to lead more effectively. Your conversation will be most worthwhile if you also decide on improvement indicators. For example, if production levels need to go up, must you become more decisive, manage subordinate performance better, or investigate inefficient supply-chain logistics? How will you prove to yourself and your boss that you have in fact become more decisive or better at performance management or improved your relationships with suppliers? Also consider setting a realistic but short time frame within which you can demonstrate improvement.

You can raise additional questions concerning your career progress over a longer time horizon in a follow-up conversation. Your objective would be to ask your superiors to identify tasks, projects, and assignments of mutual benefit to the business and to you. You also need to ask questions about how to prepare for your next assignment or next set of responsibilities. By making time and space for dialogue, you will detect which of the seven experiences to pursue, and what your organization and you will gain. This will throw light on your pathway to development in the short term, helping you to focus on either building or broadening your base of leadership skills.

Building on Current Leadership Skills: Mastery

Mastery is a progressive process in which the lessons learned from a sequence of experiences build on each other. Leadership capability is increased by building on current skills and talents. Perhaps you enjoy traveling and are curious about other cultures, or get revved up by starting something from scratch, or take satisfaction in negotiating with government officials to work through legal niceties. Your interests may match your company's interest in your becoming one of their cross-culturally savvy gurus or expert at new business startups or masterful at reaching agreements with local, state, and central government officials. The more you build, that is, the more you collect the same kind of experience, the more you will become a masterful leader, successfully guiding your company through the intricacies of your area of expertise.

Broadening Your Base of Leadership Skills: Versatility

Versatility, which is as essential as mastery, comes from excursions into new playing fields of thought and action. Leadership capability is expanded by acquiring different skills and broadening your base of skills. You may be a cross-cultural guru, but maybe you could be even more effective as a leader if you were able to inspire subordinates or skillfully execute a project. Perhaps your sound business instincts, which have led to the successful launch of a couple of ventures, must be complemented by more diplomacy with clients and media representatives. As a final example, although your strengths as a negotiator with local government bureaucrats has created record growth for your company for almost a decade, maybe your company and you will profit from your crossing over to run a manufacturing unit. The more you broaden, that is, the more you collect different kinds of experiences, the more you learn to think, feel, and act differently than before. This lets you infuse fresh insights about yourself and other people into the work at hand, making you a versatile leader.

For pressing forward as a learner, there is another useful way of applying the concepts of leadership mastery and versatility. The three lesson domains—leading self, others, and the business—are outlined in the next section. Broadly, *mastery* advances the learner along *one* domain of lessons (or even a specific lesson in one domain), and is usually about running the business. In contrast, versatility develops from fusing together lessons from the *three* domains of leading self, leading others, and leading the business. For example, a simple assignment such as opening a new office requires more than technical and detailed knowledge about facility operations (business management). Your ability to manage your own time (self-management) and work effectively with many different people (relationship management) also comes into play. My recommendation is that as you pursue experiences that teach, and learn to extract more from the experiences you are given, remind yourself to seek learning across all three lesson domains; versatile leadership is the need of the time.

Build or broaden? The two approaches are not mutually exclusive, and can be woven together. Honor your own instincts on how to shape your career. If you have had conversations with your boss, you are ready to outline a plan of action for yourself for your next step. A sample plan is included to guide your efforts and can be customized to suit your intentions (see table 8.2).[14]

BENEFITING SELF, OTHERS, YOUR ORGANIZATION, AND SOCIETY: USING YOUR LEADERSHIP LESSONS

The true worth of your learning lies in the benefits or outcomes that ripple out—from self through others to your organization and society. We focus on *how* benefits from well-learned leadership lessons can be realized, not on benefits *per se*. The three domains of lessons that were referenced in chapter 1 (see table 1.1, Opportunity Matrix) are described briefly. Then, I share ideas on how you can create multilayered benefits from the lessons you have learned.

- *Leading self* lessons relate to the inner world of leaders and effective ways to manage themselves—their thoughts,

Table 8.2 Sample plan for learning and development

Assignment:
Investigate and make recommendations on whether to outsource three business services currently operating in house.

Time frame:
February to June

Lessons to learn:
Navigate politics and gain influence—work with managers from different functions to make politically charged decisions.
Engage multiple stakeholders—gather and organize information from external vendors to prepare a credible report with recommendations for upper management.

Personal skills, behaviors, and perspectives to practice:
Learn to become objective by separating facts from opinions or assumptions.
Facilitate discussions in which conflicting points of view are heard and respected.
Become more confident by making presentations and providing recommendations to top management.

Learning tactics:
Review best-practice studies on outsourcing ("thinking" tactic).
Interview individuals in the organization involved in past decisions about outsourcing ("accessing others" tactic).
Browse in the self-improvement section of the local bookstore for books on competent communication to manage anxiety about presentation to top management ("feeling" tactic).

People to ask for guidance:
Ask my boss whether he or she will be my coach.
Identify three-to-five colleagues who are willing to be a sounding board for problem solving the issues.
Get feedback from two or three trusted vendors about whether my information-gathering processes are fair and effective.

Other practices:
Make a learning log to note what is going well or not going well, my own feelings, and what I may need to do differently.
Meditate to center myself before conducting group discussions.

emotions, actions, and attitudes. Confidence, self-awareness, and personal leadership insights are developed, which are essential to self-management.

- *Leading others* lessons relate to the world of people and involve interpersonal and social skills that equip leaders to connect with people. These include managing, motivating and developing subordinates, navigating politics, gaining influence, engaging multiple stakeholders, and cross-cultural savvy—all of which constitute the essentials of relationship management.
- *Leading the business* lessons relate to the world of running a business and facilitating the accomplishment of work in organizations. Effective execution, innovation and entrepreneurship, and functional and technical expertise are the essentials of managing a unit, department, or the organization, that is, business management.

This next observation is pivotal because it can affect your whole approach to leadership learning. Business schools and executive development programs typically instruct participants on how to run a business or an organization. Experiences, then, are the foremost and almost exclusive source of learning about oneself and others. Herein lies the power of experience—the source of lessons on leading self and leading others, which in turn are the essence of leadership.

Turning to how you can cascade the benefits of your learning through your business enterprise, several tough questions must be tackled. Do you give credence to your own learning? How do you make that visible to others? Can you elevate your learning into fruitful discussions with co-workers?[15] How do you apply the lessons you have learned to make an impact on your organization and eventually society? While noting that these questions call for a degree of thoughtfulness that is beyond the scope of this chapter, here are simple ideas to consider.

- For yourself, if you can clarify what you have learned from an assignment, you can more consciously apply your learning to subsequent assignments.
- With trusted colleagues and co-workers, if you can tell the story of your encountered dilemmas, thought processes, mistakes, and realizations, your openness will hearten others to learn from your and their own experiences.
- Within your organization, if you can set up a face-to-face or virtual forum for sharing learning from and solutions to intractable business and managerial issues, new knowledge and previously untried methods can take hold more rapidly, funneling into best practices.

The cumulative impact of this ripple of learning across the organization will unquestionably affect the future of your business organization, and thereby, economic and social progress in Indian society.

Finally, I invite you to consider that masterful and versatile leaders ultimately benefit society. In chapter 1, the concept of *lokasamgraha* was introduced. *Lokasamgraha* is woven into the fabric of traditional thinking, and has affected the outlook of Indian leaders.[16] An example of *lokasamgraha* from nature is that of the sun that gives light to all without preference.[17] In the same way, many past and present exemplary business leaders have called on themselves to dedicate their managerial work to the broad vision of nation building and service to society.

This time-honored Indian belief about the manager's role in society and business resonates with Robert Greenleaf's concept of servant leadership.[18] With Hermann Hesse's novella *Journey to the East* as catalyst for his thinking, Greenleaf came to believe that "the great leader is first experienced as a servant to others."[19] I propose that managers who have matured as leaders by dint of learning from experiences are nicely positioned to serve their organizations and society. I advocate that next-generation leaders explore their personal purpose for learning the lessons of leadership, and suggest that service to society is a distinctive ideal to follow.

Our research among business leaders in India (to quote a colleague) confirms that "managers today are active consumers of diverse experiences. This represents a significant shift for leadership development—from a top-down instruction-based paradigm towards a learner-centric and experience-based approach to developing leaders."[20] We are all enrolled in the school of life, and "experiences" are our curriculum. As we advance on our career pathways, there are experiences that we intentionally seek and bring upon ourselves, and other experiences that our destinies bring to us. Many and varied, each is opportune. By engaging holistically—with heart, head, and spirit—with our experiences, we release our own latent talent for leading.

In concluding, my wish for you the reader, and for myself, is that we continue to be blessed by the wealth of powerful experiences. By trekking along the pathways of powerful experience, we become composed, and can confidently consecrate our actions to serving others and our organizations. In the end, what counts are not our feelings, thoughts, and words, but our deeds, by which we come to be respected as leaders creating the future.

ENDNOTES

1. S. Jobs, You've Got to Find What You Love. Commencement address delivered on June 12, 2005. Available at http://news-service.stanford.edu/news/2005/june15/jobs-061505.html.
2. Adapted from Essential Program Principles for CCL. *Ability to Learn: The New Core Competency*. Internal document. (Greensboro, NC: Center for Creative Leadership, 1995).
3. M.W. McCall, *High Flyers: Developing the Next Generation of Leaders* (Boston: Harvard Business School Press, 1998).
4. A. Huxley, *Texts and Pretexts: An Anthology of Commentaries* (London: Chatto and Windus, 1932).

5. S. Caldwell, Available at http://thinkexist.com/quotes/sarah_caldwell/.
6. 360 BY DESIGN. A proprietary tool for 360-degree assessment owned by the Center for Creative Leadership (Greensboro, NC, 2009).
7. C. S. Dweck, *Mindset: The New Psychology of Success* (New York, NY: Ballantine Books, a division of Random House, Inc., 2006).
8. D. A. Kolb, *Experiential Learning: Experience as the Source of Learning and Development* (Englewood Cliffs, NJ: Prentice Hall, 1984).
9. M. A. Dalton, *Learning Tactics Inventory: Participant Workbook* (San Francisco: Jossey-Bass, 1999).
10. J. Stein (editor in chief), *The Random House Dictionary of the English Language: The Unabridged Edition* (New York, NY: Random House, 1967).
11. F. Cohen & R. S. Lazarus, Coping with the Stresses of Illness. In G. C. Stone, F. Cohen & N. E. Adler (eds.), *Health Psychology* (San Francisco: Jossey-Bass, 1980); K. A. Bunker & A. D. Webb, *Learning How to Learn from Experience: Impact of Stress and Coping* (Greensboro: NC: Center for Creative Leadership, 1992).
12. K. Lewin, *Resolving Social Conflicts: and Field Theory in Social Science* (Washington, D.C.: APA, 1997); J. Mezirow, *Transformative Dimensions of Adult Learning* (San Francisco: Jossey-Bass, 1991); I. G. Sarason, B. R. Sarason, & J. H. Johnson, *Stressful Life Events: Measurements, Moderators, and Adaptation*. (Technical report #CO-OO1) (Arlington, VA: Office of Naval Research, 1980).
13. J. Yip, *Return on Experience: Learning Leadership at Work* (Greensboro, NC: Center for Creative Leadership, 2009).
14. Adapted from C. D. McCauley, *Developmental Assignments: Creating Learning Experiences Without Changing Jobs* (Greensboro, NC: Center for Creative Leadership, 2006).
15. Yip, op. cit.
16. Readers interested in an in-depth understanding of *lokasamgraha* are referred to the works of S. K. Chakraborty and S. P. Agarwal as referenced in chapters 1 and 8 respectively. For example, Chakraborty cautions that the concept aims at cosmocentric consciousness, and should not be bounded by the standpoint of social ethics, for which the context is sociocentric consciousness.
17. S. P. Agarwal, *The Social Message of the Gita Symbolized as Lokasamgraha* (New Delhi: MLBD, 1995).
18. R. K. Greenleaf, *The Servant as Leader* (Cambridge, MA: Center for Applied Studies, 1970).
19. L. Spears, Practicing Servant Leadership. In *Leader to Leader*, no. 34, Fall 2004, 7–11.
20. Yip, op. cit.

Appendix

THE LESSONS OF EXPERIENCE—INDIA RESEARCH PROJECT

This appendix provides an overview of the Lessons of Experience research program, the Lessons of Experience—India (LOE–India) study, methods of interview analysis, and initial findings, as well as concluding remarks. The information is for academics and students with an interest in a) using qualitative methods for leadership research or b) extending the LOE methodology to study leadership development in other sectors—such as the government, nongovernment organizations (NGOs), and small and midsized enterprises; or other populations—such as women and social entrepreneurs.

LESSONS OF EXPERIENCE RESEARCH PROGRAM

The Lessons of Experience study started in the summer of 1981 as a collaborative project between six large U.S. corporations and three Center researchers. The study had a practical objective—its aim was to investigate how executive talent could be developed for running businesses in years to come. Based on interviews and surveys of 191 senior executives, the CCL researchers gleaned the key developmental events in executives' lives and the lessons learned from those events. The research findings were reported in *Lessons of Experience: How*

Successful Executives Develop on the Job.[1] In following years, these data and findings were used to develop two instruments, a program for HR managers, and several modules that are part of the Center's current portfolio of products and programs.

As the managerial ranks in the U.S. became more diverse, and began to include women, African-Americans, Hispanics, and Asian-Americans, additional studies were conducted to investigate their experiences and lessons learned.[2] Outside of CCL, the same research methodology was applied to examine the experiences of international executives[3] and business executives in the Netherlands and Japan.[4]

In 2003, CCL extended the LOE research globally, with comparable interview and survey data gathered in the U.S., India, Singapore, and China.[5] An overview of the most relevant studies is shown in table A.1.

THE LOE-INDIA STUDY

This project was jointly undertaken by the Tata Management Training Center (TMTC) and CCL–Asia, due to the valuable knowledge to be gained on developing and managing the talent pipeline in India. Eight global Indian corporations were selected as research sites. The criteria used to finalize our sample of organizations were that the companies be: a) homegrown and global; b) headquartered in different regions in India; c) representative of several industry sectors; and d) comparable in size and reputation. At our invitation, and with the help of key individuals in HR groups, each company nominated 10–15 top and senior leaders for 60–90-minute in-depth, on-site interviews. (See chapter 1, table 1.2, and table 1.3 for demographic information.)

Before the interviews, each study participant was provided with background information about the project and its sponsors, and an Interview Guide. The preliminary materials noted

Table A.1 Overview of Lessons of Experience studies

Country	*Year completed*	*Number of participants*	*Organizations*
China	2009	54	Four state-owned and two private-sector companies
Singapore	2008	36	12 government ministries and 18 government agencies
India	2007	71	Eight global private-sector companies
United States	2005	354	Participants in CCL's *Leadership at the Peak* program. From this sample of senior executives, 72% were U.S.-based, and 28% were internationally based.
Global (36 countries)	1999	101	16 global private-sector companies
United States	1996	288	Participants in CCL's leader development programs
United States	1985	76	25 *Fortune* 100 companies
United States	1984	191	Six *Fortune* 100 companies

that data privacy and confidentiality are guiding principles at CCL. Study participants were asked for their permission to tape-record and transcribe their interview. They were assured that their name would not be used in publications, nor the name of their company disclosed without express permission.

The semistructured interviews used the following format:

- Looking back over your career, what are the three key events or experiences that had a lasting impact on you and influenced how you lead and manage today?
- What did you learn from these events or experiences?

To validate and extend the data, three general questions were included in the interview:

- What would you say is the most significant thing you've learned as an adult—the one thing you'd pass on to someone else if you could?
- What advice would you give to a younger manager, someone just starting out?
- What is the biggest challenge you are facing as a leader now, or expect to face in the next few years?

The interviews were conducted by a primary team of three researchers, and a secondary team of three leadership development professionals. (All participated in a four-day workshop, designed by CCL's senior research faculty, on the LOE research methodology.) During initial data collection, interviewers worked in pairs to ensure that the research team used a consistent approach to conducting the interviews. Subsequently, individual researchers traveled to different regions of the country to complete data collection.

METHODS OF INTERVIEW ANALYSIS

More than 100 interviews were taped and transcribed (including the pilot study), and yielded 71 usable interviews. The mandate for the Indian research team was to develop its own set of event and lesson codes to take advantage of an emic perspective and allow cultural differences to emerge.

There are three ways to develop themes and codes: a) theory driven; b) etic, or prior data or research driven; and c) emic, or inductive and data driven.[6] We opted to combine an emic and etic approach—using inductive, data-driven analysis in the first two stages, and results from previous and parallel research for the analysis in the third stage. These three stages are described in the following.

Stage One

The first stage of analysis included the following activities.

1. *Independent coding*. Each researcher-identified event and lesson quotations and themes and assigned provisional codes for each interview. Importantly, experiences from which no lessons were learned were not coded; and conversely, lessons that were not anchored in an experience were also not coded.
2. *Team discussion*. Agreements about how to resolve discrepancies between coders were developed. This consisted of group process guidelines and decision rules.
3. *Team coding*. Discrepancies were resolved, and non-usable data discarded. Discrepancies were resolved by majority. If two of three coders agreed on a code, that code was assigned. If two of three coders could not agree, then the event or the lesson were dropped. (Statistically, intercoder agreement of the codes accepted for further analysis was at least 67 percent.) Provisional codes developed by each researcher during the independent coding activity were discussed and revised as needed, with the objective of developing a common codebook for consistent coding of the remaining interviews.

Stage Two

The second stage of analysis (occurring after approximately one-third of the interviews had been analyzed) involved developing codes, code definitions, completing the coding, uploading the interview data into the qualitative data analysis software Atlas-TI for further analysis and interpretation, and developing an Event–Lesson matrix. Details follow.

1. *Code development*. Themes from *each* quotation were reviewed and grouped to create separate bundles of event

and lesson quotations. This group process involved considerable discussion. After all team members had agreed on the exclusive and exhaustive bundling of quotations, code definitions were developed for each bundle.

2. *Code definition and codebook development*. Well-written code definitions make it possible to code more precisely. Our aim was to write codes that were clear and concise labels that were precisely related to the data, and conceptually meaningful for describing the phenomenon at the core of each event or lesson. Each code definition included: a one-to-three sentence summary statement; examples (drawn from the themes and quotations); and contextual information to help differentiate one coding category from another coding categories when necessary. Codes and code definitions were reviewed and revised as needed, after respectful discussions involving a full spectrum of perspectives and opinions. The codebook, a compilation of all the event and lesson codes, became a reference guide for coding the remaining interviews. To avoid duplication of efforts, one researcher was appointed as editor for creating and updating the codebook.
3. *Completing the coding*. The remaining interviews were coded, with iterations between individual and team coding. The constant comparison method of qualitative analysis was used, due to which codes and code definitions continued to be reviewed and revised.[7]
4. *Using Atlas-TI for analysis and interpretation*.[8] Since this qualitative data analysis tool is useful for managing large bodies of textual information, 71 interviews were uploaded. Quotations or chunks of data identifying an event or lesson were marked; themes noting one central topic or idea per quote were entered; and codes from the codebook were assigned. To maintain data integrity, one researcher was given responsibility for maintaining and updating the

Atlas-TI database, although all the researchers were able to access the database. Reports generated by Atlas-TI were used as a starting point to analyze relationships between experiences and lessons, and to discern meaningful patterns of learning.

5. *Developing an Event–Lesson matrix.* The objective of the analysis was to uncover whether in the Indian business context, certain experiences were more likely to produce specific learning. Interview data analysis had resulted in 26 event codes and 29 lesson codes. A matrix was developed, linking every event with all lessons learned. By determining which events and lessons were a) cited most frequently relative to other events and lessons, and b) cited by the highest percentage of interviewees, a second version of the original matrix was developed. Intended to present the most relevant findings concisely, the second version, or Opportunity Matrix (see chapter 1, table 1.1) is the basis of this book.

Stage Three

Currently in progress, the third stage of analysis uses an etic approach, and involves comparing the India codes and definitions with those from recent LOE studies in the U.S., China, and Singapore. The team is cross-cultural and includes researchers from each country-based project. The code comparison across countries is leading to the identification of country-based unique codes and similar codes with country-based nuances in the data. The comparison is also surfacing similar data with different code names and definitions, which raises questions about culturally tinged shades of meaning for the codes *per se*.

The intent of this analysis is to uncover meaningful variations across countries and industry sectors, and produce useful generalizations. We hope to use the analysis for theory development, and to connect broad categories of events with the most salient leadership lessons they teach. Specifically, in connection with the LOE–India project, we expect this analysis to help us discern the ways in which the experiences and lessons of Indian business executives may be similar or different from that of executives in other countries and industry sectors.

FINDINGS

The LOE–India study generated arrays of data which have been analyzed, interpreted, and summarized in the report *Developing Future Leaders for High-Growth Indian Companies: New Perspectives.*[9]

Here, I focus on the highlights of the *initial* analysis, primarily using tables, figures, and brief explanations. As shown in figure A.1, in the India study, the raw data pool (from the interviews) included 309 quotations of key events (later relabeled "experiences") and 575 quotations of lessons learned from those events. Based on the qualitative data analysis (as described in the preceding section) the 26 event codes were

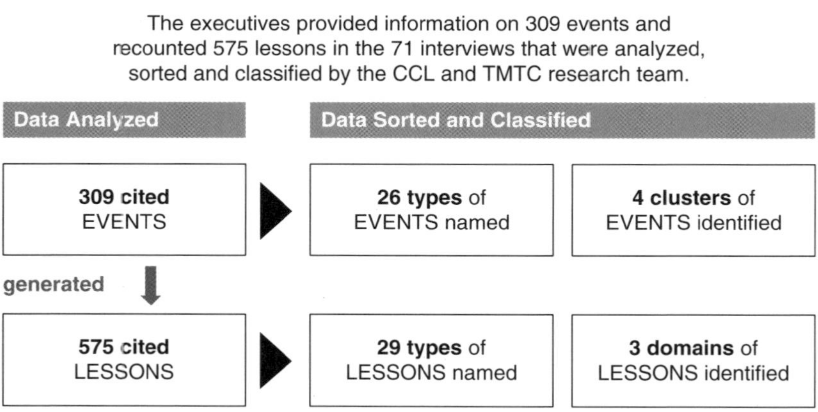

Figure A.1 Overview of analysis

categorized into four clusters, and the 29 lesson codes were categorized into three domains.

Event Clusters and Events

The four broad event clusters that comprehensively include all the experiences described by business leaders in India are as follows:

- *challenging assignments*, which come from a posting, promotion, or task assigned to the manager by their company. The assignment is typically difficult and sometimes requires struggle. Different kinds of assignments sharpen different leadership abilities. Challenging assignments were cited by 49 percent of interviewees
- *inspiring superiors and bosses*, who directly and indirectly support (or do not support) learning and the learner. Their influence is possibly more powerful than they themselves realize. Inspiring superiors and bosses were cited by 17 percent of interviewees
- *adverse situations*, which are imposed by the environment. Usually, the difficulties experienced during the event are not within the control of the company or its executives. Adverse situations were cited by 10 percent of interviewees
- *personal events*, which include personal career and life choices, and life experiences. Excluding "early job experience" and "coursework and training," these events are usually outside company control. Core lessons are learned that influence leadership aspirations and performance. Personal events were cited by 23 percent of interviewees.

The 26 types of events, clustered as above, are displayed in table A.2; the 11 events that were most widely cited are marked with an asterisk.

Table A.2 The variety of experiences of Indian senior executives

Challenging assignments	*Inspiring superiors or bosses*	*Adverse situations*	*Personal events*
New initiative*	Positive role model or superior*	Mistakes*	Early job experience*
Fix-it or turnaround*	Boss who coaches*	Dealing with labor and trade unions	Coursework and training*
International assignment*	Catalyst boss*	Business crisis	Early life experience
Lateral or cross-functional move*	Negative role model or superior	Experience of ethical violation	Personal experience
Increase in job scope*			Role models (nonwork)
Managing organizational change			Cross-organizational move
Negotiation			Working for a non-Indian MNC
Supervisory responsibility			
Cross-organizational collaboration			
Rural assignment			
M&A			

*Top 11 events

Note that discussions with Indian clients and the broader community of CCL researchers has led to the renaming of event clusters, the merging of some event types, and the reclassification of some event types from one cluster to another. For example, "inspiring superiors or bosses" was renamed "developmental relationships" and "role models (nonwork)" event was reclassified into this cluster. (See Van Velsor, McCauley, and Ruderman for details.)[10]

Also, as a result of presentations to several companies participating in the study, the format for sharing the findings has been simplified over time, while remaining true to the data. This is illustrated by the pie chart in figure A.2. The pie chart displays the frequency of citation of each of the seven essential and "other" experiences as a percent of all 309 experiences cited. The pie chart clarifies that while

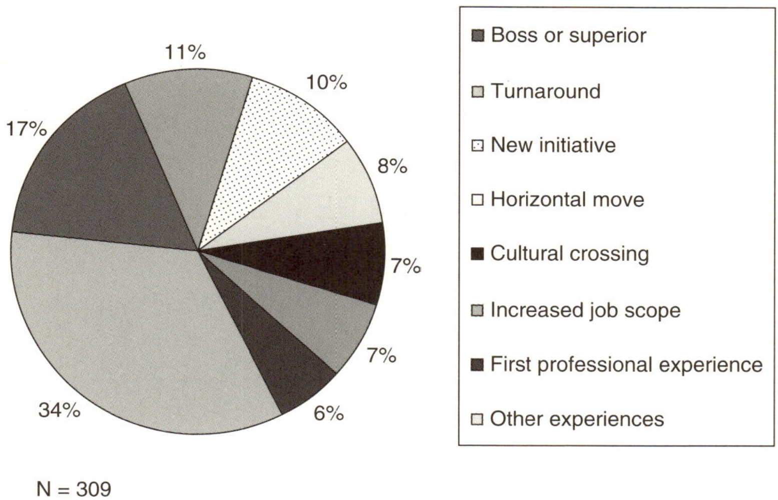

Figure A.2 Seven essential experiences (based on frequency of citation of the event as a percentage of all 309 events cited)

the seven essential experiences described in this book account for 65 percent of all experiences, there are a variety of other experiences that are cited far less frequently, but aggregate to 35 percent of all experiences from which leadership lessons are learned.

In other words, the research results have been reframed to convey the important "rules of thumb" that business organizations can apply most easily. The "other" experiences (excluded from discussion in this book) from which leadership is learned are: business crisis; coursework and training; dealings with labor and trade unions; early life and personal experiences; ethical violations; mergers and acquisitions; mistakes; negotiations; and nonwork role models.

Lesson Domains and Lessons

The three broad lesson domains were described in chapter 8. Here we include a display of the 29 lessons learned by business leaders in India, classified by lesson domain; the 11 lessons that were most widely cited are marked with an asterisk (see table A.3).

CONCLUDING REMARKS

The LOE–India research methodology can be applied to study how leadership development occurs among other populations of leaders and in other organizational sectors in India. We invite research colleagues in India and from other countries to refine and adapt this methodology as needed. Additional studies can be opportunities for theory development, hypothesis testing, in-depth case studies, action research, and other exploratory and foundational enquiry. We hope you become interested in replicating and extending this work, and in securing the institutional support to do so.

Table A.3 The variety of lessons learned by Indian senior executives

The meaning of leadership		
Leading self	*Leading others*	*Leading the business*
Confidence* Self-awareness* Understanding and committing to life goals* Integrity* Becoming humane Dealing with setbacks Developing flexibility and adaptability Seeing things from a new perspective Dealing with ambiguity	Managing and motivating subordinates* Developing subordinates* Team management* Cultural savvy Building relationships with peers and seniors Building credibility Communication and feedback Gaining influence Managing multiple stakeholders	Execution and operating savvy* Innovation, creativity, and entrepreneurship* Functional and technical knowledge* Gathering information, knowledge, and insights* Decision making and problem solving Acquiring a broad organizational view and strategic insight Customer orientation Handling organizational and cultural change

*Top 11 lessons

ENDNOTES

1. M. W. McCall, Jr., M. M. Lombardo, & A. M. Morrison, *The Lessons of Experience: How Successful Executives Develop on the Job* (San Francisco: New Lexington Press, 1988).
2. C. A. Douglas, *Key Events and Lessons for Managers in a Diverse Workforce: A Report on Research and Findings* (Greensboro, N.C.: Center for Creative Leadership, 2003); A. Morrison, R. P. White, & E. Van Velsor, *Breaking the Glass Ceiling: Can Women Reach the Top of America's Largest Corporations?* (Updated ed.) (Reading, MA: Addison-Wesley, 1992).
3. M. W. McCall, Jr. & G. P. Hollenbeck, *Developing Global Executives: The Lessons of International Experience* (Boston: Harvard Business School Press, 2002).

4. F. Brave, *Learning for Leadership: A New Look at Management Development*. Colloquium held at the Center for Creative Leadership, Greensboro, N.C., July 2002; Work Institute Recruit Company, "*The Lessons of Experience" in Japan: Research Report* (Tokyo: Work Institute Recruit, 2001).
5. R. Conway, E. Van Velsor, & C. Criswell, *Learning from Experience: Critical Life Lessons of Senior Executives*. Academy of Management Conference, Atlanta, GA. August 11; M. Wilson, *Developing Future Leaders for High-Growth Indian Companies*. Technical Report (Center for Creative Leadership, 2008); J. Yip & M. Wilson, *Developing Public Service Leaders in Singapore*. Technical Report (Center for Creative Leadership, 2008); Y. Zhang, A. Chandrasekar, & R. Wei, *Developing Future Leaders for Chinese Companies*. Technical Report (Center for Creative Leadership, 2009).
6. R. E. Boyatzis, *Transforming Qualitative Information: Thematic Analysis and Code Development* (Thousand Oaks, CA: Sage Publications, Inc., 1998).
7. B. G. Glaser & A. L. Strauss, *The Discovery of Grounded Theory* (Chicago: Aldine, 1967).
8. Atlas.ti. Available at http://www.atlasti.com/.
9. M. Wilson, *Developing Future Leaders for High-Growth Indian Companies*. Technical Report (Center for Creative Leadership, 2008).
10. J. Yip & M. Wilson, M. Learning from Experience. In E. Van Velsor, C. M. McCauley, & M. Ruderman (eds.) *The Center for Creative Leadership Handbook of Leadership Development* (third edn.) (San Francisco: Jossey Bass, 2010), 63–95.

Index

About the Center for Creative Leadership

The Center for Creative Leadership (CCL) is a top-ranked, global provider of executive education that unlocks individual and organizational potential through its exclusive focus on leadership development and research. Founded in 1970 as a nonprofit educational institution, CCL helps clients worldwide cultivate creative leadership—the capacity to achieve more than imagined by thinking and acting beyond boundaries—through an array of programs, products, and other services.

Ranked among the world's top providers of executive eduction by *Bloomberg BusinessWeek* and the *Financial Times*, CCL is headquartered in Greensboro, North Carolina, with locations in Colorado Springs, Colorado; San Diego, California; Brussels, Belgium; Moscow, Russia; Singapore; Pune, India; and Addis Ababa, Ethiopia. Supported by more than 450 faculty members and staff, it works annually with more than twenty thousand leaders and two thousand organizations. In addition, 12 network associates around the world offer selected CCL programs and assessments.

CCL draws strength from its nonprofit status and educational mission, which provide unusual flexibility in a world where quarterly profits often drive thinking and direction. It has the freedom to be objective, wary of short-term trends, and motivated foremost by its mission—hence its substantial and sustained investment in leadership research. Although CCL's work is always grounded in a strong foundation of research, it focuses on achieving a beneficial impact in the real world. Its efforts are geared to be practical and action oriented, helping leaders and their organizations to achieve their goals and vision more effectively. The desire to transform learning and ideas into action provides the impetus for CCL's programs, assessments, publications, and services.

Capabilities

CCL's activities encompass leadership education, knowledge generation and dissemination, and building a community centered on leadership. CCL is broadly recognized for excellence in executive education, leadership development, and innovation by sources such as *BusinessWeek*, *Financial Times*, the *New York Times*, and the *Wall Street Journal*.

Open-Enrollment Programs

Twelve open-enrollment courses are designed for leaders at all levels, as well as people responsible for leadership development and training at their organizations. This portfolio offers distinct choices for participants seeking a particular learning environment or type of experience. Some programs are structured specifically around small-group activities, discussion, and personal reflection, while others offer hands-on opportunities through business simulations, artistic exploration, team-building exercises, and new skills practice. Many of these programs offer private one-on-one sessions with a feedback coach.

For a complete listing of programs, visit http://www.ccl.org/programs.

Customized Programs

CCL develops tailored educational solutions for more than a hundred client organizations around the world each year.

Through this applied practice, CCL structures and delivers programs focused on specific leadership development needs within the context of defined organizational challenges, including innovation, merging cultures, and developing a broader pool of leaders. The objective is to help organizations develop, within their own cultures, the leadership capacity they need to tackle challenges as they emerge.

Program details are available online at http://www.ccl.org/custom.

Coaching

CCL's suite of coaching services is designed to help leaders maintain a sustained focus and generate increased momentum toward achieving their goals. These coaching alternatives vary in depth and duration, and serve a variety of needs, from helping an executive sort through career and life issues to working with an organization to integrate coaching into its internal development process. Its coaching offerings, which can supplement program attendance or be customized for specific individual or team needs, are based on its model of assessment, challenge, and support (ACS).

Learn more about CCL's coaching services at http://www.ccl.org/coaching.

Assessment and Development Resources

CCL pioneered 360-degree feedback, and believes that assessment provides a solid foundation for learning, growth, and transformation, and that development truly happens when an individual recognizes the need to change. CCL offers a broad selection of assessment tools, online resources, and simulations that can help individuals, teams, and organizations increase their self-awareness, facilitate their own learning, enable their development, and increase their effectiveness.

CCL's assessments are profiled at http://www.ccl.org/assessments.

Publications

The theoretical foundation for many of its programs, as well as the results of CCL's extensive and often groundbreaking research, can be found in the scores of publications issued by CCL Press and through the center's alliance with Jossey-Bass, a Wiley imprint. Among these are landmark works, such as *Breaking the Glass Ceiling* and *The Lessons of Experience*, as well as quick-read guidebooks focused on core aspects of leadership. CCL publications provide insights and practical advice to help individuals become more effective leaders, develop leadership training within organizations, tackle issues of change and diversity, and build the systems and strategies that advance leadership collectively at the institutional level.

A complete listing of CCL publications is available at http://www.ccl.org/publications.

Leadership Community

To ensure that the center's work remains focused, relevant, and important to the individuals and organizations it serves, CCL maintains a host of networks, councils, and learning and virtual communities that bring together alumni, donors, faculty, practicing leaders, and thought leaders from around the globe. CCL also forges relationships and alliances with individuals, organizations, and associations that share its values and mission. The energy, insights, and support from these relationships help shape and sustain CCL's educational and research practices, and provide its clients with an added measure of motivation and inspiration as they continue their lifelong commitment to leadership and learning.

To learn more, visit http://www.ccl.org/community.

Research

CCL's portfolio of programs, products, and services is built on a solid foundation of behavioral science research. The role of research at CCL is to advance the understanding of leadership and transform learning into practical tools for participants and clients. CCL's research is the hub of a cycle that transforms knowledge into applications and applications into knowledge, thereby illuminating the way organizations think about and enact leadership and leader development.

Find out more about current research initiatives at http://www.ccl.org/research.

For additional information about CCL, visit http://www.ccl.org or call Client Services at (336) 545-2810.

Seven Experience

Pathways to Lea

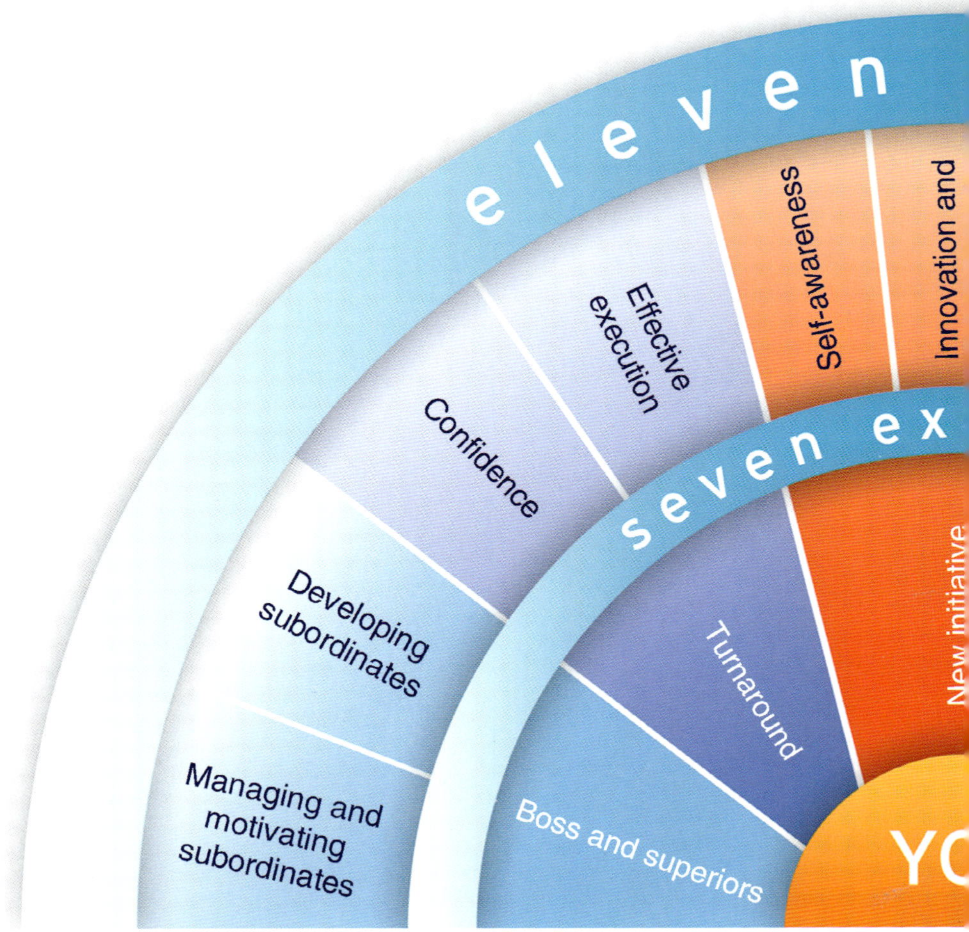

Note: Based on the *Lessons of Experience—India* research, t
in Chapter 1, page 10, labelled as Figure 1.1.

s, Eleven Lessons

der Development

his image can also be found

Center for Creative Leadership
www.ccl.org